Other People's Words

Other People's Words

*Friendship, Loss, and
the Conversations
That Never End*

Lissa Soep

**Spiegel
and Grau**

S&G

Spiegel & Grau, New York
www.spiegelandgrau.com

This is a work of nonfiction. The stories in the book reflect the author's recollections. Some names and locations have been changed to protect the privacy of people involved. In the personal correspondence that is included, tiny edits have been made here and there for concision and clarity. Some dialogue has been recreated from memory.

PERMISSIONS
Thank you to Max and Sadie (Jonnie's children), Jeanne and Pete (Jonnie's siblings), David (Christine's brother), Chas (my love), and to Mercy and Emily, who have given me permission to share their writing and stories and whose friendship means the world.

Permission granted to reprint from *The Dialogic Imagination: Four Essays* by Mikhail Mikhaïlovich Bakhtin, edited by Michael Holquist, translated by Caryl Emerson and Michael Holquist, Copyright © 1981 by the University of Texas Press.

Excerpts from "At the Fishhouses" from *POEMS* by Elizabeth Bishop. Copyright © 2011 by The Alice H. Methfessel Trust. Publisher's Note and compilation copyright © 2011 by Farrar, Straus and Giroux. Reprinted by permission of Farrar, Straus and Giroux. All Rights Reserved.

Jacket design by Gabriele Wilson
Interior design by Meighan Cavanaugh

Library of Congress Cataloging-in-Publication Data Available Upon Request

ISBN 978-1-95411-835-5 (hardcover)
ISBN 978-1-95411-836-2 (eBook)
Published in the United States of America

First Edition
10 9 8 7 6 5 4 3 2 1

To Christine and to Jonnie

Between languages, there was a wordless territory where everything was still unnamed, and, therefore, nearly eternal. Meaning was all there was. And language was doubled, and also erased.

—INGRID ROJAS CONTRERAS,
The Man Who Could Move Clouds

Other People's Words

Itaru Sasaki bought the phone booth before the tsunami hit in 2011, before thousands of people were killed or went missing from towns like his along the coast of Japan. He had set up the booth in his garden to talk to his cousin, who had recently died. It was painted white, with paned windows and a tiny, pale green roof of oxidized shingles. Itaru closed himself into the booth and dialed up his cousin using the heavy black rotary phone inside. He called it *kaze no denwa*, the wind telephone. It carried his words on the wind.

Then came an earthquake under the sea and its catastrophic waves. Soon grievers other than Itaru showed up in his garden to use the wind telephone. They dialed numbers for destroyed lines that didn't ring in ruined houses.

"Hello."

"I'll be in fourth grade."

"Grandma's fine."

"I started tennis in junior high."

"Everyone is waiting for you," one man said on a call to his wife, years after she'd disappeared. "I'll build the house in the same place. Eat something—anything. Just be alive, somewhere, anywhere."

The man hung up and stepped back into the world. Like glimpsing the precise profile of a lost lover on the face of a stranger until, inevitably, the figure in the crowd takes back its own outlines. Like waking from a dream of your dead father brushing your bangs from your eyes. I wonder if the people on the other end of the phone stay the same age despite the passing years, how the conversations change over time.

Callers listen for voices, remembered and longed for, and produce two sides of a half-uttered conversation that is at once ordinary and magical. Feeling the weight of the receiver in their hands, the visitors say hello, fiddle with the cord, its length a kind of evidence that a connection is being made and with it, the split-second possibility of a person picking up. The silence on the other end of the line is an opening to conjure the vital words of others. The living keep shaping their language around the voices of their dead. At least their lost ones aren't all-the-way gone anymore, for as long as the conversations last.

I had two friends, Christine and Jonnie. Christine exited slowly, Jonnie all at once. Again and again, I have sought them out in places that give voice to those who are missing. Places like Itaru's booth, or just my own wild mind making sense of a world without my friends.

This is what many of us do when we've lost someone we love. We tune into split seconds that stretch open and fill with voices, real and imagined. In grief, our voices find life through the dialogues they contain.

It was a twentieth-century Russian scholar, Mikhail Bakhtin, known for his expansive philosophy of language, who taught me to notice layers of dialogue within our words, conversations humming with voices beyond those who are with us in the here-and-now. My relationship to Bakhtin formed along the edges of his books, through notes I crammed into the margins over decades. With time, Bakhtin evolved from a thinker I studied to a spirit presiding over my deepest loves and losses. He showed me that it's possible to daydream other people's words into existence, to form speech out of silence. From Bakhtin, from Christine, from Jonnie, I discovered something essential: that language is teeming with voices, past and present, unruly and inexhaustible. That our words hold an "inner infinity," which is itself a consolation.

You should come soon," Mercy said. I heard her moving around in the background, restless, probably doing lunges in her kitchen. "She's barely got any words left."

We had arrived at the moment we'd known was coming, after all these years with Christine's words and stories. At least Mercy was here for it. Her possible absence had been Christine's greatest fear. At least we'll be together, all four of us. That's what Christine wanted more than anything.

It was so strange, that a call this somber could unleash a surge of pointed energy. Something inside of me came awake, in possession of the permission I needed for everything else to fall away. There were frequent flyer accounts to empty and last-minute sleepovers to arrange for the kids. Chas and I filled our suitcases and emailed our bosses to say we'd be out for a few days, checking items off lists with unusual efficiency but in a daze, too, spiraling into a version of time that kept turning back on itself, through sudden spells of remembering. It felt like more than remembering. Scenes that had grown still and distant in my mind came rushing toward me, reanimated and full of color.

Mercy told me to bring pictures. She said Christine seemed to respond to them, that she looked from the photo to the person who handed it to her, as if she were taking in some kind of meaning, working out a connection. I went from drawer to drawer in the house, collecting photos that we'd stashed here and there over twenty years or thumbtacked to a bookshelf in the living room. I was used to the sensation by then—from all the times I'd dug around for a receipt or safety pin and stumbled across messages from Christine: a series of postcards page-numbered in the corner, lines of her cursive, a xeroxed poem. Pausing to absorb what I'd found, I never knew which voice of hers, which phase of her, I would read.

There was her easy smile, in a photo from eighteen years prior, in 1997, at the first apartment Chas and I rented in San Francisco. In it, I've got my arms around Mercy and Christine, and Mercy's holding up a card I'd painted as a going-away present when the two of them were moving back east: a little watercolor with our four faces crowded into an oval of flowers. From our wedding album, I peeled out a picture taken after the ceremony—Mercy and Christine holding paper plates and licking frosting off their fingers, twin short haircuts, their heads tipped toward each other, seemingly unaware of the camera. In the black desk where I wrote my dissertation, I found a blurry one of Christine and me on the orange couch we still have, and I could tell by the shape of my face that I was pregnant. In a different drawer: an image of Chas and Mercy bundled into fleeces and hats on the deck. I vaguely remembered having stashed that one deep in a pile so the kids wouldn't come across evidence of Chas smoking a cigarette. There was one of Mercy, Christine, and me in bathing suits gripping a rock wall, ankle deep in a Big Sur river.

I was inside these pictures and outside of them, sliding them into a manila folder and watching myself in this larger choreography, already playing out what I would say when I saw Christine and what it would feel like when she said nothing back.

Mercy and I were in our twenties when we met in a grad school class in 1996. She was working on a master's in education, and I was in the same department for my PhD. It was fall in the Bay Area, and she was deeply tan. Mercy worshipped the sun, still does. Her black hair was cropped short and pushed up from her forehead in the front. She wore a soft white T-shirt with brown stitching around the collar, and if it sounds like I was attracted to her: yes. A thin brass bracelet slid up her arm when she raised her hand to ask a question. She asked a lot of questions.

I watched her from across the seminar room and found myself thinking about her outside of class. I was food shopping, or dozing off partway through a reading, and my mind went to her brash intellect and the taut muscles that flexed up and down her forearms when she wrote. After we started getting lunch sometimes, I noticed the way she asked me unexpected questions and seemed taken by my answers, how our eyes met when someone in the class made a pretentious comment, how a weathered leather belt sat low across the expanse of her hips. Soon, there was that feeling—nervous, gorgeous, and rare: the sense of choosing and being chosen. And it didn't take long for me to realize that Mercy was someone lots of people fell in love with. I did and didn't for two reasons. One, I was already with Chas. Two, she told me about Christine.

The four of us arranged to get together at a bar called the Rite Spot in the Mission. They kept the place dark, tiny white candles in glass cups flickering on the tables, people getting up to play a piano in the back of the room. Christine was twenty years older than the rest of us, which gave her a kind of silver-haired mystery. She and Mercy lit each other's cigarettes.

On the sidewalk at the end of the night, I watched the two of them make their way to the dusty station wagon they'd driven cross-country and realized that I needed to start reshaping whatever feelings I had for Mercy into friendship with the two of them.

Before long, Chas and Christine called each other on the phone to talk about books and soccer games. He and Mercy went running and picked up spring rolls for dinner. I still felt the heat of her arm when she shoved the gear shift into position on the freeway carpooling us down to campus from our apartments in the city. Moving around the kitchen with her, slicing shallots into translucent ribbons and tossing them in a sizzling skillet, sometimes I let myself imagine what it would be like to have a life with Mercy for myself, for it to be Mercy joining my family gatherings, the two of us choosing furniture for a place of our own, her hands on my skin. I oscillated between wanting some undeniable touch or talk to happen between us and liking it better to hold desire for myself. And then Christine called out from the next room to see what time the food would be ready, or Chas came in to set the table, and I snapped back to our real arrangements. The four of us fell into a friendship that was no less a love-of-my-life because it crisscrossed two couples and didn't last.

Mercy sat down at Café Flore in the Castro to write Christine a birthday card. "If we could not write, would our tongues spell out sentences in each other's mouths?" she asked in the first line. This was still early in their relationship, a time that lent itself to ardent poetry.

They'd met at a high school where Mercy was an intern, fresh out of college. The mentor she was assigned was a reserved, wiry, salty older white woman whose stature in the English department was obvious, in the way colleagues stopped what they were doing and listened when she addressed the room: Christine. When Christine recited essays at assemblies that offered slanting glimpses into her life beyond school, students devoured the details and tried to write like her, *be* like her, mine their own lives for stories, like one Christine wrote about gathering with her family to scatter her father's ashes into the sea.

> They stood, uncertain, on the solid planks. She stared at her mother's clenched fist, holding what was only father to her but . . . husband and lover, companion of years before she was even born, with history she never knew, with conversations in mornings and evenings, tears of their own making, cherishing all memory now. And her

mother flung to the wind what was left of the man in a gesture of bravery and promise. And they watched and waited, bent over the railing, suspended in grief and time and wonder. Something flashed in the water. Husband, father, grandfather—him: translated into color, brilliant and rapid as lightning. Glitter. Delicate, piercing, holy, stupidly chemical, all she could know of life-after-death. She held it in her hand, surprised by the grit and weight and rough edges of what was and couldn't be her father.

Mercy and Christine's relationship began with teaching and coaching, and writing was always there. They exchanged lesson plans and lines from Audre Lorde, personal disclosures and teasing suggestions, and then an invitation to the river on a Sunday when neither had dorm duty and they kissed under a tree and full moon. They waited a long time to tell anyone at school, and when Mercy visited her parents in Pennsylvania, she didn't tell them either.

remember that what your parents don't know/don't want to know is, nevertheless, a good/healthy/deep/mysterious/ passionate part of your story . . .

Most nights, they took out stationery or yellow legal pads and hand-wrote letters to all sorts of people. Former students, old relatives, a school administrator or politician who'd done something they took issue with. And they wrote to each other.

and the Monday light is beautiful, at this time of the evening, and the citronella candles smell like summer . . .

When they spoke about love, they avoided the word. It embarrassed them if anyone called them lovers. They shared an unspoken, definitive resistance to certain expressions, including "I love you." "We worked really hard to avoid that phrase," Mercy told me. "A lot of the language that was between us was designed to name something we didn't say. The absence of 'I love you' in our lives was a language."

They moved into a house together near school. Specific numbers mattered to them, and they took pictures anytime they came across them—like one of their ages stenciled on a post of the Golden Gate Bridge. They called random things mister, like Mr. Teapot or Mr. Duffle Bag. On a small blackboard in the kitchen, they left notes each day. "Good morning," Christine wrote in white chalk. "I'm heading off. ♥ C."

Christine took a sabbatical so she could join Mercy in the Bay Area for her year of grad school. Their closeness intoxicated me, the way they patterned their looks, language, and sensibilities on each other. I stopped wearing eyeliner and wrote "ahhhh" in books to mark my favorite passages, like they did on student papers. Chas teased me about it.

"You hanging out with M and C today?" he said over the rim of his mug, taking in my bare face and the loose tank top I'd picked up from a thrift shop and tucked into the front of a pair of old Levi's.

"Ha ha. Wasn't that you smoking a clove cigarette last weekend?" I said back, looking pointedly at the book he was reading—Christine's recommendation. We were both doing the same thing.

In an anthropology class, Mercy and I learned about Bakhtin's essays on dialogue and his role in a broader "linguistic turn" within twentieth-century social theory. Our professor explained that Bakhtin and other scholars in the movement believed that any philosophical problem could be solved or dissolved through language, by closely studying ordinary speech in art and everyday life. In class, I filled a notebook with the professor's words and little drawings of the other students around the table in the seminar room, including one of Mercy in circle glasses with tiny hoop earrings and the sleeves of her V-neck sweater pushed up to her elbows. Carpooling to campus, I pulled Bakhtin's book *The Dialogic Imagination* out of my bag and read lines out loud while Mercy drove.

"Our speech is filled to overflowing with other people's words," Bakhtin wrote, and I sensed that this was an idea I could live by, a way to understand how intimacy and conflict take root within speech, a vibration that's always there. I listen to a singer covering another artist's song and experience both of their voices at once, a devotional chord. I say something and hear my mother in the cadence (or Chas does, and looks vaguely panicked). Bakhtin was obsessed with dialogue, and so am I. We both listen for it not just in the usual sense of conversation between people, but in the many voices that lace through a single person's words.

Like many of Bakhtin's contemporaries, he was interested in language as a system, but Bakhtin stood out for his attention to the particularities, the textures and accents that distinguish our voices. He noticed how a novel's narrator can pick up vocal patterns from its protagonists, how the author's own voice can shimmer in and out of the text without overtly announcing itself. He saw these same qualities in ordinary speech, too, calling them instances of double-voicing.

For Bakhtin, a "conversation of the most intense kind" is a monologue that is really a dialogue. One person is talking, but their words engage with something vital outside themselves, beyond their limits: the imagined voice of a silent speaker, who enters the dialogue as a hidden, hovering participant. Sometimes, as a haunting.

Conversation like this can take hold when we're talking to someone else or even inside our own heads. I'm playing with my sister's kid, one of those babies who's always being called an old soul. "She's like, 'You've got to be kidding me!'" I say, producing a knowing personality long before this child is old enough to have one. Or, I'm sweeping up one afternoon and catch myself embroiled in an imagined argument, speaking both sets of angry lines that are suddenly more real than the floorboards beneath my feet. The intensity of these conversations has to do with the remixing of time and place. An outside voice can be beckoned or break in like a burglar. Where we are and with whom matter less than whose voices echo through the utterances, whose ideas and histories resonate through what is said and heard. Inside our words, we are never without companions.

To me, this is more than an idea. It is a liberation. Because once we accept that no one absolutely possesses even their own speech, that it's filled to overflowing with the words of others, then voices and texts that were once closed crack open. They are capacious and mysterious, alive with new interpretations. I am always saying more than the words that come out of my mouth. I can always find new meanings in what others say to me. When a loved one's voice diminishes or goes silent, after a relationship is destroyed or some-one dies, I still carry the voice and keep hearing it.

Roma had an early soccer game that morning in 2012. She and my other daughter, Simone, were in pajamas at the breakfast table, spooning cereal into their mouths. They were ten and six, and between bites, they used the necklines of their tops to wipe their faces, leaving behind milky lip and nostril prints.

I went upstairs, first in line to take a shower, when my phone rang. It was a friend from college. "I have terrible news for you," she said. I remember those last two words: "for you." It was confusing that she'd said "terrible," because "for you" made the news sound, to me at least, like it might be good.

"There's been an accident. Jonnie died," my friend said.

"What are you talking about?" I yelled at her, immediately feeling bad for using such a ferocious tone.

Jonnie had been swimming in a lake in Montana. The drivers of a boat didn't see him and its motor severed his leg. He had been only 150 feet from the shore, heading to a rock that his wife, my friend Emily, had been swimming to since she was little.

"Chas, get up here right now."

Emily and their two kids were just yards away from the lake's stony shore, in a hot tub with Emily's sister, when a cousin came running.

"Chas, Jonnie died."

Emily raced to the edge of the water where people were trying to save him, but it was too late.

"Already, there was no trace of him," wrote Jonnie's sister, Jeanne, about swimming in that same water the day after he died. "The lake and the shore were all the same for having taken his life."

Trying to register the awful details, I flashed back to my conversation with Emily just a few days before the accident. She had called to tell me that her stepfather had died. He'd been hiking near his home in Montana when he lost his footing and slid off the trail down the side of the mountain. He didn't survive the fall. Emily was close to her stepdad, but her older child's seventh birthday was that week, and school had just started. She couldn't figure out if they should fly to Montana and called me to talk it through. Ultimately, she and Jonnie decided it would be too much, that they would stay in Cambridge, mourn the loss together from home. But then, family members from all over the country started gathering at Flathead Lake, talking and telling stories, and Emily and Jonnie realized they had to be there. So they went.

When Jonnie was a little kid, he went camping at Mount Rainier, and his tent was struck by lightning. Volts of electricity shot through his body, leaving him permanently hard of hearing in one ear. When he died, I kept thinking that he'd survived a lightning strike but not an afternoon swim.

For years when we lived in the same San Francisco neighborhood in our early thirties, Emily and Jonnie came over on Thursday nights for dinner, and then all four of us piled into our queen-sized bed to watch TV, sharing updates on whatever was going on in our lives during the commercials. Emily and I had become friends a decade earlier, before I went to California, when we both moved to Cambridge after graduating from college. We were introduced by her cousin, my housemate senior year. Emily had been a dancer growing up, good enough to earn a spot with a professional ballet school in New York when she was a kid. But even that young, she knew her body would never fit within the punishing constraints of the classical dance world and neither would her temperament, so she turned down the offer. She liked modern better anyway, the stomp and spread and athleticism of it, the flexed feet and sense of abandon.

One Saturday, she convinced me to take a technique class with her at a studio in Central Square, where she rehearsed with her dance company. I'm not sure what she was thinking, bringing me along. "Why not?" she said. "It'll be fun!" When it was time for each of us, one by one, to execute a complex sequence diagonally across the floor, she did so gracefully. I missed the first step and stumbled through the rest of the choreography. When I made it to the opposite corner, face burning, Emily laughed and pulled me in for a sweaty hug. "Don't feel bad!" she insisted. "It's an advanced class!" We went to my place for dinner, ate pasta, and sprawled on the couch. She extended her long, strong leg over to my side of the sofa. "Oooooh, how about a foot rub?" she cooed through a massive smile that poked a perfect dimple into each of her cheeks. There was no saying no to her.

Around the time Emily and I were becoming friends, her dad had been living with kidney failure for almost twenty years. For the entire duration of her childhood, he self-dialyzed at home, a five-hour routine that involved connecting himself via a series of tubes to a bathtub-shaped appliance three times per week. "From my point of view, I was lucky," Emily once wrote about growing up with her dad's illness. She got her dad's undivided attention the whole time he was attached to the machine. They played chess or watched TV in his small Manhattan apartment, and she didn't realize there was anything unusual about her situation until she was six, when a friend came over one day and freaked out when she saw the tubes filling with blood. "Wait," Emily had said, "your dad doesn't do this, too?"

In 1992, he needed a transplant. Emily and her older sister, Sara, whom I was also friends with, decided that one of them would give their dad a kidney. How do you make a choice like that, at twenty-two? Which daughter takes on the pain and risk of the procedure and a life with only one kidney left? Which sister gets to experience the intimacy and power of having essentially saved their dad's life? Finally, a blood test showed that Emily was a better match with her dad by a barely detectable measure, and that fact made the decision for them. I sent a bouquet of purple anemones to the hospital and told her how amazing she was. She was hearing that kind of thing a lot and told me that she appreciated all the love and support—but that we were missing something. "Yes," she said. "I did it for him. But I also did it for me."

Once Emily and her dad recovered from their tandem surgeries, she got her life back. She no longer had to worry, each time her phone rang, that he was back in the hospital, or worse. After a few years doing odd jobs around Texas and Mexico, she moved to New York to study social work. That's where she met Jonnie, at a friend's wedding. He fell for Emily immediately. It took her a little more time. When she called to tell me about him, she described his bright orange hair and massive laugh and said that he had an MBA and worked in business. She'd never dated anyone who worked in business and wasn't sure she wanted to. But then, they were kissing on the couch in her tiny Manhattan studio, and Jonnie paused to ask if she would take a boat ride with him in a river halfway around the world, and she said absolutely. She was starting to understand his mix of sweetness and sense of adventure, which seemed to foretell a freewheeling and meaningful life. By the time they got together, Jonnie had been arrested eleven times in various countries. He'd been part of ACT UP in the eighties and organized demonstrations for racial justice and against police corruption. He'd protested military spending and joined the anarchist wing of the Great Peace March to walk across America for nuclear disarmament, calling himself "Jonnie Vermont" because he'd lived there for a spell. An arrest outside an abortion clinic to protest Operation Rescue landed him in his hometown paper in Stockton, California, while his mother was running for mayor. When Emily told me about these parts of Jonnie's life, I said I really wanted to meet this guy, and soon enough, I did.

Emily and Jonnie moved to the Bay Area where his family lived, and by this point, I was there, too. She joined a therapy practice. Jonnie got a job in real estate. They found an apartment just over the hill from Chas and me, in Bernal Heights.

Their wedding took place on the deck of a museum overlooking the bay. I worked with Karen, Emily's cousin who'd introduced us, to weave together a chuppah out of jewel-toned ribbons to match Emily's wine-red dress. Emily and Jonnie vowed to see the world together. At the reception, they danced to "Always a Woman to Me," Jonnie's choice, with choreography Emily had ripped from a movie, and Jonnie—unlike me in the studio back in Cambridge—didn't care that his performance was, how shall I say, not exactly perfect. Then, during the toasts, one of Jonnie's old friends, a writer at a local weekly, approached the front of the ballroom in a rumpled blazer, carrying a carousel of slides. He proceeded to tick through so many images of their anarchist days together that Jonnie's brother, Pete, had to pull the plug and practically force the guy back to his seat. I knew that in this crowd—in most crowds, if I'm honest—I was on the square side of the guest list, in my flowery sundress and pedicure, with my exceedingly limited drug experiences and overdeveloped fear of getting in trouble. Listening to Jonnie's friend's insistent narration as he clicked through image after image of their direct actions, I sensed the resentment seething just below the surface, the mix of anger and hurt when he slinked back to his table laid out with plates of chicken and asparagus and a pretty bouquet at the center. He was losing Jonnie Vermont—to this? But, taking in the scene, Jonnie Vermont just let out his outrageous, full-bodied laugh. Jonnie Vermont was an anarchist who went to business school and didn't sweat the contradiction.

Chas and I hosted a brunch in our living room the morning after the wedding. Roma wasn't yet two, and when the party was over, Chas and Jonnie pushed plates and cups into garbage bags, and I put Roma in the kitchen sink, where she liked to putter around in a few inches of water with a trickle running from the tap.

Emily and I sat down on the floor nearby, and when Emily rested her head on my legs, I started playing with her hair. Spotting us entwined like that, Roma suddenly clamored to her feet in the basin, her soft baby body glossy from the water, and pointed indignantly at me. "Mine!" she screeched. She wouldn't sit down again until Emily extricated herself from my lap. The dynamics among us shape-shifted, our bodies and intimacies realigned, all from the force of a single word. I wondered what lesson Roma took from the moment.

Emily and Jonnie often took Roma along to the farmers' market or on a walk around Bernal Hill. They were our only friends who swept Roma into their lives like that. We were more than happy to hand her over, and I sensed that their time together as a threesome was a chance for Emily and Jonnie to practice what it felt like to pass a baby back and forth, spoon purees from tiny jars, change a diaper on the cement floor of a public restroom. Once, Chas and I were totally worn down from trying to break Roma's pacifier dependency, so we were especially grateful when Emily and Jonnie took her to the park. Pulling up in front of our house a couple of hours later, they were proud of how well it had gone. But we had forgotten to mention the pacifier thing, and when Chas went to unbuckle Roma's seat from the back of the car, she was sound asleep and sucking away on one that we'd failed to remove from an inner pocket of her diaper bag. We laughed later, knowing someday when they had kids, they'd understand how disproportionately devastating a setback like this felt, in the state of exhaustion produced by raising children. One Sunday when I was out of town, they had people over, and Jonnie convinced Chas to bring Roma and a jug of margaritas, which was great until she shat through her diaper while strapped to Chas's chest. Drunk and miserable, he headed home with a soiled shirt and cranky baby, and Jonnie just roared. "You laugh now," Chas said. "Just you wait." We were already writing a story for them, mapping a plot into a future we were certain we would share. We never considered that Jonnie would only get to be there for the beginning.

By the time Emily and Jonnie had their own babies, Max in 2005 and Sadie two years later, Emily and Jonnie had moved back to Cambridge, and soon, three of their four parents were sick in some very serious way. Both of their mothers had developed cancer, and three weeks after Emily's mom died on the East Coast, her father was admitted to the ICU in Berkeley. After nearly eighteen years with Emily's kidney, he'd suffered strokes, a heart attack, and eventually dementia. When I met up with her at the hospital, Emily asked if being there was too upsetting for me, seeing him in the bed with a breathing tube down his throat. I'd just been watching Emily and Sara hustle down the hospital hallway, fetching nurses and taking phone calls in matching yoga pants. I wondered if they'd subconsciously dressed like twins, the way they sometimes used to as little kids. I wondered if matching like that was a way of remembering and holding on. I'd seen Sara ease earbuds into her father's ears and play Louis Armstrong from an iPad, and how— wordless—he stared into her eyes and beamed. It didn't feel too upsetting for me. But once Emily asked, I worried that maybe it should have. I wasn't sure what it told me about myself, that I didn't want to leave.

Over those years with small children and dying parents, Emily and Jonnie were often exhausted by the end of the day from all the stress and caregiving. And yet, there were still plenty of sweet moments, like the time she was pregnant with Sadie and a song she liked came on the radio while she was cooking in the kitchen. She started dancing, and the exaggerated curves formed by the growing baby made her slow-motion swaying that much more beguiling. Jonnie relished her unencumbered pleasure. "There you go," he said, laughing. "Yeah, shake it, mama, shake it, mama. Ha!"

After he died, Emily showed me videos she'd recorded on her phone. There was one of Jonnie with Sadie in a pool. She was four years old. This was a month before the accident. They'd buried three parents in four years, and things were finally supposed to be easing up. Sadie, in pigtails, had shed her floaties and bathing suit. With one hand, she gripped the pool's edge, and with the other, she reached for Jonnie.

"Get your feet up on the wall, Sades, so you can push off," Jonnie said, his voice serious, his attention entirely trained on her. "Go!"

She launched from the edge. "Paddle, paddle, paddle!" Jonnie urged, and she did. "That's good stuff, Sade," he said. He caught her in his hands and then delivered her back to the edge for more.

Mikhail Mikhailovich Bakhtin was twenty-six years old when he fell in love with a librarian, Elena Aleksandrovna Okolovich. In 1921 they married and moved in together in a small flat in the town of Vitebsk, a center for intellectual life and culture. She had cared for him through a bout of typhoid, and as soon as he'd recovered, the two resumed his habit of inviting friends over for gatherings that could extend through the night, the apartment filling with cigarette smoke. The newlyweds and their friends argued over language, poetry, music, ethics, religion, books, politics. Rounds and rounds of dialogue about dialogue.

A writer. A pianist. Philosophers of religion, language, architecture. None of them had any idea at the time that their ragtag group would someday be described as a "Circle" with a capital C: the Bakhtin Circle.

The Circle's freewheeling intellectual conversations would soon become dangerous. As the years went by, the friends would learn to finesse their writing through abstraction or Marxist references, so they didn't fall out of line with the Soviet regime. But back then, crowded around a table in the apartment living room, they were just a gathering of confidants, with their notebooks and nascent ideas, who couldn't get enough of each other's company.

Bakhtin was called *chudak*, which meant "funny man," even "idiot," a term of endearment. His own writing was mostly unpublished at the time—notebooks filled with hand-scrawled ideas, some fragments and some carefully formulated paragraphs. He wrote and wrote whenever he could, except when his illness made writing impossible.

Just before he got married to Elena Alexandrovna, Bakhtin was diagnosed with chronic osteomyelitis, a bone disease that had plagued him since childhood. When the condition flared, high fevers, skin lesions, and terrible pain relegated him to bed for months at a time. It went on like that for almost twenty years, until Bakhtin was in his forties and had his right leg amputated at the knee. From then on, he used wooden crutches to get around and finally experienced lasting relief.

The Circle had been meeting for eight years, in Nevel, Vitebsk, and eventually Leningrad, when Bakhtin was arrested on Christmas Eve, 1928. He'd been part of a secret society that wasn't properly registered, and their discussions of religion and philosophy made him a target. There's a scene in the Julian Barnes novel *The Noise of Time*, set in a later period, where the secret police arrive in the middle of the night to drag Russian intellectuals, artists, and dissidents in pajamas from their beds, forcing them to dress while the scowling officers cradle their guns. It's what I imagine Bakhtin and his friends might have feared each night when they headed off to sleep. After his arrest and days of interrogation, Bakhtin received a five-year punishment of hard labor at a concentration camp on an island in the White Sea near the Arctic Circle. This was a death sentence. A man with his condition would never survive.

Together with Bakhtin, Elena and their friends launched a campaign to get his sentence commuted to exile. Her husband's disorder was the most powerful weapon they possessed in the fight for his survival. That, and a letter signed by the writer Maxim Gorky, which Elena had obtained through a friendship with his wife. There was also a well-timed review from a Bolshevik who approved of a book Bakhtin had recently published about Fyodor Dostoevsky's novels. Dostoevsky's characters, Bakhtin wrote, were "free people, capable of standing alongside their creator, capable of not agreeing with him and even of rebelling against him." Free also, at least for the time being, was Mikhail Mikhailovich Bakhtin.

The Bakhtins set out not for the gulag but for Kazakhstan, where, he later wrote, they were surrounded by "people half-dead from hunger on the streets . . . children blue in the face." He worked for years as an accountant, reporting once a week to the police. Instead of giving academic talks on literature or philosophy, he lectured pig farmers in exchange for food and tobacco.

Due to his pain, Bakhtin was routinely confined to the bed or couch. This was true before his exile and after, when he and Elena moved from town to town. And so, all of those scholars, artists, and students who wanted to spend time with Bakhtin had no choice but to come to him.

If he hadn't been sick, Bakhtin might have gotten a steady university job, and though he and his friends had long been interested in dialogue, he might not have felt, in his bones, its power to emancipate people from dehumanizing conditions, like the very circumstances that defined so much of his own life. He might not have recognized in words a capacity for the world not to "coincide with itself," for people living in ailing bodies or hostile societies to discover a realm where experience and memory can flow and fade with boundless life. I wonder if, from within his condition of confinement and exile, dialogue was an escape for Bakhtin, a man contending with chronic illness and an oppressive government, who created evenings so convivial that no one wanted them to end, his friends talking and talking until the sun came up.

Spring break, 1997, rolled around for Mercy and me. The four of us decided to go away. We knew this was our only chance before Mercy and Christine headed back to New Hampshire. We wanted to go someplace special. I knew exactly where.

A few years prior, when Chas and I had been in the swoon of our own early days together, we took a road trip down the California coast. When we came upon a detour sign before merging onto Route 1, for some reason we ignored it and drove on for a couple of hours before hitting the mudslide the sign had warned about. It was getting dark, and I sat there calculating with dread the extra hours of backtracking we'd just added to our trip.

I spotted lights up ahead and thought there might be a store with a bathroom, figured I'd better use it while I could. But it wasn't a store. It was a compound of cabins outfitted with old furniture and down comforters, and a restaurant that served salsa so fresh, you could tell the corn had just been cut from the cob because some of the rows were still intact. It was a magical place in a magical place—Big Sur, California, a misty village tucked into cliffs that tower over sandy beaches along the Pacific. This place felt about as far away in vibe and location as I could get in America from the town outside of Hartford where I grew up, with my mom and sister, in a colonial house with waterbeds, shag carpets, and a plastic sprinkler that spit water all summer onto a narrow grass lawn.

Chas and I couldn't stay over then, but we did find out that rooms were ninety-five dollars a night—totally doable for a weekend trip with Mercy and Christine to celebrate finishing finals. Wearing ridiculous sunglasses, the three of them showed up at the computer lab on campus where I was tweaking a bibliography. Mercy had turned in her last assignment and they were tired of waiting, so they dragged me out.

When we got to the beach, Christine, Mercy, and Chas charged into the water without regard for the crashing currents or freezing cold, dropped their shirts and shorts along the way for me to collect into a pile while I watched from the sand, their bobbing shoulders and slicked-back hair shining in the sun. I didn't mind watching from a distance. I was scared of the surf, hadn't played sports since a mortifying extramural season of soccer in fourth grade, was raised in a family where everyone was in therapy and Jewish. They ducked underwater and swiveled their heads around to locate one another across the ripples and foam once they came up for air.

We had given ourselves an assignment to read *Lolita* and talk about it over the weekend. Back at the inn, we took hot showers and bundled up so we could drink wine outside on the deck in the woods, the sun low in the sky, the thinnest branches lit from behind into line drawings in the air. Mercy handed smokes to Chas and Christine. The burning clove mixed with the forest smells, the soil and bark, the ocean. Christine bent her knees to form a surface of her thighs for her copy of the book, defaced with markings from all the times she'd taught it at school. The feeling among us was still so new. We didn't really talk about *Lolita* that evening, though. There was too much else to say.

"If we could not write, would the contour of our legs entwined together be parentheses or a slash?" That's the second line of the poem Mercy wrote for Christine's birthday, not long before our trip to Big Sur. At the time, not writing to each other felt inconceivable, an idea to play with in a love letter. But now, when I think of that line in the poem, I flash forward to Christine seventeen years later, alone on the snowy sand of a winter beach in Maine, on a call with me, gusts of wind blowing across the surface of her phone.

"You have to stop," I told her. "You can't keep writing to her."

And then later, I told Mercy, "You can't say anything that will give her even a shred of hope. It will only hurt her. Otherwise, I swear she will never let you go."

There's Daddy's bag," Emily's seven-year-old child said when they spotted Jonnie's suitcase on the conveyor belt at the San Francisco airport. This was a couple of days after the accident. Emily and her two kids had flown in to be with Sara and Jonnie's siblings and father. I'd borrowed a minivan to pick them up. Emily dragged the bag behind her to the van. Loading the luggage into the trunk, I started to tell her a memory of Jonnie and she shook her head and looked away. "I can't," she said. "I can't fall apart right now." Later that evening, she picked out one of Jonnie's button-downs and gave it to me for Chas. She handed me one of Jonnie's T-shirts so I could wear it that night, next to her in bed. I rubbed her head and hoped to God that the warmth of our bodies would bring out the smell in his shirt, so that maybe she would sense him in the haze of her fitful movement in and out of sleep.

"Where is he? No, really, like where actually is he?" Emily kept asking, in the days, weeks, and months after he died. Seeking an answer, she went to the Apple store at the mall and beseeched a salesperson—calmly, then desperately, then furiously—to unlock parts of Jonnie's phone, so she could retrieve whatever traces of his voice were trapped inside, blocked by a password she couldn't believe she didn't know. She played back his words, again and again.

"I look for you everywhere," she wrote in a letter to him. She had so many questions.

> I went on a four mile run in 15 degree weather and wore your pants and balaclava hat to keep warm . . . It is still so unbelievable to me that you died. How did this happen?
>
> Nothing is right, and frankly although our lives were so stressful and full of struggle these last years with all the other deaths and illness, I want it all back. I want you back and even the bickering at night about telling me to get off the computer so we could talk.
>
> And I wonder all the time if you know I am so sad without you. Do you feel us? See us? Is your spirit nearby?

There was a memorial service in Cambridge, a month after Jonnie died. Sara gave out stones she'd collected from the Montana beach so each of us could hold one in our hands. When two friends with guitars sang "Farewell Reel" by Patti Smith, I looked at Emily in the front row, head in her hands, her kids being cared for by a friend in a separate room, and I thought: In this hall filled with hundreds of people, how can she feel anything but entirely alone? Chas stepped onto the stage and told a story about their wedding brunch at our house. Jonnie had just finished cutting lemon slices into half circles and arranging them delicately on a plate of lox when Roma sneezed a huge mess of snot all over her face. Jonnie reached over and scooped it up with his bare hand.

"It's one of those disgusting things you do for your own child," Chas said at the podium. "But it's a special kind of person who would do that for someone else's snot-nosed kid. He seemed to be thinking: 'Wash my hands later, right now is an opportunity to deliver some love.'"

Jonnie's sister, Jeanne, said Jonnie was the only person besides her husband whom she wanted at her child's birth, and that it was only because he was on an overseas trip when she went into labor that he'd narrowly missed seeing his sister's vagina. Jeanne's husband said a lesson from Jonnie's life was to play with other people's children, and I thought of the time we spent the weekend with him in Point Reyes. He was bouncing Roma up and down on his lap so she could see her face in the mirror that hung above him, until he got going so fast that he smacked her little forehead hard against the glass—"Oh, no, Roma! Oh no!"—and then laughed his ass off while she howled. Pete talked about spotting his brother once, hitchhiking along the side of the road, and when he pulled over and offered to take Jonnie home for a meal, he was like, "Nah, I'm busy." There were many, many stories of the 1958 Ford school bus Jonnie and a ragtag group of friends lived in after college. One of those friends called Jonnie a great conversationalist, especially when he was speaking both sides of the conversation. It struck me, listening to the speeches, that it's normal for people to become larger than life when they die young, but Jonnie was larger than life when he was still alive.

We kept invoking Jonnie's voice, even as we started to absorb what it meant to have lost him. We were reaching for ways to hold him close, to feel him beside us, for his death not to be the end of his story. Bakhtin had a word for this sense of infinite, open-ended becoming: "unfinalizability." I thought about this possibility all through the service, running my thumb over the cold surface of my stone. For Bakhtin, to treat any human experience, even death, "as if it is all here, in its entirety . . . without a way out of this bound-edness," deprives that experience of its open-ended future and inner truth. "It is denied freedom." One image in particular came to me. Bakhtin said that limiting ourselves to monologue, to a single voice, meaning, or context, is the equivalent of imprisoning ourselves in a dungeon. I didn't want to think of Jonnie locked away, apart from the rest of us, in the dark, alone.

After the speeches and songs, the service ended with a slideshow of pictures. What I remember: Jonnie, a little boy, with his brother and sister in a forest. A teenager in ripped purple tights that he'd mended with nail polish, eyes shining, his unwashed orange hair zigzagging to his waist. On the front page of a newspaper with a bandana covering his face, in the thick of a roiling crowd. At a sunny breakfast table with Emily and his kids, wrinkles in the moon-white skin around his eyes.

When the slideshow came to an end, we filed out of the hall and a bunch of us piled onto a couch. Emily's brother-in-law came over with a camera.

"I have to take a picture," he said, "so we have it for the slideshow at the funeral for whichever one of us dies next."

And with those words, he set us off into two dimensions at once. Mercy calls a time like this "a present moment full of itself and full of tomorrow." Time travel is one of the ways that language gives life. Even after a person falls silent, their words remain wide open, in dialogue with the world. "Only that which exists in itself can die," Bakhtin wrote, and he believed that none of us exists that way, apart from others. "Even meanings born in dialogues of the remotest past will never be finally grasped once and for all." At some point in the future, these meanings will be renewed by more dialogue. "Nothing is absolutely dead: every meaning will someday have its festival of rebirth." For Bakhtin, even death is but an incomplete departure.

In the months after Jonnie died, when I visited, I watched Emily pack the kids' lunches, bundle them into jackets and mittens— "Let's go, Sadie, we're gonna be late!"—and hustle them through the cold to school. Then she'd come home and slow way down, shuffle papers around in drawers, pick up an envelope or flyer to scan the words, but I couldn't tell if the meaning was coming through. It was almost as if she wasn't looking for a permission slip from school or a solid plan for spring break but for the person she was supposed to be figuring all this stuff out *with*.

On Halloween that first year, she dressed up Sadie as a dog and Max in a shiny orange wig. "I'll be a black widow," she said, half-joking, imagining a head-to-toe black outfit and eight arms springing from her back, the kind of thing that would make Jonnie laugh. Then they trick-or-treated toward Dudley Street, now "Deadly Street," where residents had transformed every front porch into an epic death scene hung with bloody, cut-off arms and legs. Emily whisked her kids in the other direction and later emailed a strongly worded note to the neighborhood association saying that maybe, the next time they picked a theme, they might consider how their holiday decorations would affect children who'd experienced violence or loss. Meanwhile, Emily kept writing to Jonnie. In April:

Today's your birthday. Maxine and Sadie insisted we make your cake. I thought it was a good idea but then felt really unsure and upset. No candles. No song. We just eat it?

It was so frustrating, she said, when she couldn't remember something—whether Max had gotten the shot they needed, the name of the Thai place with the good noodles—and Jonnie wasn't there to fill in the gaps.

Sadie asked how old you were today. I told her 47. She just listened. I see your smile and twinkly eyes as I think of how you looked at her and Maxine. And hear your booming laugh and voice. I hear you saying, "Maximo."

Joan Didion wrote that grief can feel a lot like suspense, and I thought of Emily, searching for something—*Where is it? Where is he?* Our words dig grooves: question, answer, question, answer. We've spent our whole lives in that rhythm, until one day, the answer doesn't come. Will never come. And yet: the answer can be most powerful *before* it has been spoken out loud, when it exists only in the negative space of anticipation, tugging, tugging, tugging on the words that came before, words like the ones forming Emily's questions, circling without a place to land.

Word by word, language produces time rather than merely existing within it, propelling us toward what's to come, creating its own momentum. In doing so, it can fool us into believing that our lives will carry on as we thought. "Every word is directed toward an answer," Bakhtin wrote. The word can never escape "the profound influence of the answering word that it anticipates." When the possibility of an answer goes away, the word is at a loss, and so are we.

Still, dialogue doesn't stop. When the possibility of an answer went away, Itaru Sasaki installed a wind telephone in his backyard and then opened it up for visitors he didn't even know, so they could call family members swept away by a tsunami. Across the Pacific Ocean from Itaru's garden, in the Fruitvale neighborhood of Oakland, California, a police officer shot and killed Oscar Grant III on New Year's Day, 2009, and thirteen years later, at a gallery in New York, visitors stepped into phone booths that a group of artists had decorated with names and pictures. Inside, they recorded happy birthday messages for Grant and other sons and daughters killed by police. The artists turned from silence to conversation, mourning to celebration, "from death to life."

Wind telephones are portals into life-giving dialogues, and in this sense, words are booths. They contain and register our losses and form ways for us to carry on.

When Mercy was getting ready to graduate in 1997, she and Christine packed up their apartment near Golden Gate Park and headed back east. They couldn't fit all their stuff in the station wagon, so they donated anything useful to Goodwill and handpicked some items to leave behind for Chas and me. One was Bakhtin's *The Dialogic Imagination,* a paperback with a creased, dark purple cover.

"Carbonell, San Francisco," Mercy had written, her last name in blue ballpoint pen, and below that, under two thin green lines: "For Lissa—because Language Matters . . . even if I don't understand Bahktin" (or, apparently, know how to spell his name).

Mercy got a new job at a school in Massachusetts and commuted to be with Christine in New Hampshire every weekend. On Monday mornings, before leaving to head back to her work, she would sit at the kitchen table to write a note in a black bound book that the two of them had picked out for this very purpose, so Christine would have the message to read over breakfast. In that same spot, Mercy sometimes wrote to others, too.

Dear Lissa, The other day I was weeding through the papers I have stacked higher than you all over my floor + I found a letter you had sent with an article. And there was your handwriting—hoops and curves I had not seen in awhile, year-old information/news but a page to me from you. "Someone," I thought, quoting E. Bishop, "loves us all." And again, I wished I were there.

The letter went on to say that Mercy was feeling "assaulted educationally" by a colleague who'd filed a complaint over her refusal to grade papers, a practice she was committed to from her prior school. She'd been called into a meeting with the head of the English department for a talking-to.

And so I am trying to think of how I am going to enter this meeting, how you would—somehow ready with a diplomatic tone. Can I pull that off, I wonder? So, on Thursday, I will pray for your tone of voice. I miss the daily doses of you.

That last line reminded me of something that Bakhtin had written, about intonation being the most "supple" dimension of language to conjure social dynamics. For him, language exists on the borderline between the self and other. "The word in language is half someone else's. It becomes 'one's own' only when the speaker populates it with his own intention, his own accent." It is not, after all, from the dictionary that we discover our words. They exist in other people's mouths. From those dialogic origins, we find our words, feel them out, see what they can do, make them our own. And then we send those words back out into a flow of dialogue that shapes what's possible for other people to say, feel, and be.

It's like in a movie, when music from within the fictional story world of a scene jumps the narrative barrier and becomes part of the cinematic soundtrack. Imagine a mother, driving, her daughter in the passenger seat. They're fighting, then sullen, until a song comes on the car stereo. The mother starts singing along. The daughter glares out the window, brooding, but eventually, she joins in, begrudgingly at first, then all in. The two keep singing until they arrive at their destination and the mom cuts the engine. But instead of the song stopping, the music lifts up into the film's score and sustains over the daughter's exit from the car, her walk through the courtyard and into the crowded hallway of school. Sound that was once inside the scene now produces the scene. Sound experienced by two characters in the story becomes a dimension of the story. And you feel it, watching—that split-second sensation, when you realize the music leapt from a contained element to a shared soundscape. It's the moment you realize the story is bigger, wilder, more transcendent than it seemed.

After three years teaching in Massachusetts, Mercy finally got a full-time job back at the school where she'd been mentored by Christine. This meant that the two of them would once again be in the same department. For more than a decade, Christine had been one of just two or three openly queer members of the faculty. At one point during Mercy's first stint at the school, a group of kids asked the two of them to come out publicly, as an act of solidarity. Mercy told me that when administrators got wind of the plan for an upcoming assembly, they called the two of them in for a meeting. "Are you sure you're ready?" they asked Mercy, again and again. *Are* you *ready?* Mercy wanted to reply, but she held her tongue. One of the administrators wondered if they would need extra counselors on hand, in case students got upset. "We have assemblies about nuclear war and toxic waste," Christine shot back through her teeth. *No one was bringing in counselors for presentations to kids about the end of the world, but they needed counselors for this?* Christine was furious. And of course, she and Mercy went through with the assembly. They performed the coming-out event as a game show—the next year, they went with a lip-sync routine to a song by the Judds—and Mercy told me that she got letters from students five and ten years later, telling her how much the assemblies had meant to them before they'd been ready to come out themselves.

Chas and I flew to Massachusetts to spend a week at the beach with his parents. We stopped in Providence on the way, and Mercy and Christine drove down to see us. We chose a coffee shop as the meeting place and planned to sit outside on the patio. But then, enormous purple-black clouds rolled in and it started to pour. "Oh wow," I said to Chas, "remember this? Warm rain!"

We ran with our coffees and scones and ducked into the back of Mercy's truck. The roof kept us dry, but the back was open so we could hear the full effect of the rain stabbing the metal over our heads and feel the mist on our bare legs and faces.

Many years later, after everything had fallen apart, Chas convinced me to read *Crossing to Safety* by Wallace Stegner. He promised that the book wasn't going to destroy me like Stegner's other novels. It's the story of an enduring friendship between two couples who meet when they're just starting out, the husbands both professors in an English department. The book chronicles their intertwining dreams and regrets as the friends have children, chase careers, experience illness, and ultimately face death. Stegner's happy novel. Describing friendship, he wrote:

> It is a relationship that has no formal shape, there are no rules or obligations or bonds as in marriage or the family, it is held together by neither law nor property nor blood, there is no glue in it but mutual liking. It is therefore rare.

Reading Stegner's lines, I thought of the four of us in the back of Mercy's truck.

> There it was, there it is, the place where during the best times of our lives, friendship had its home and happiness its headquarters.

One of Bakhtin's dear friends, the Marxist linguist Valentin Nikolaevich Voloshinov, was so devoted to their relationship that Voloshinov moved to Vitebsk in part so he could care for Bakhtin through his bouts of pain, even choosing his apartments based on which locations would allow him to get over to Bakhtin's place quickly in case of a medical crisis. A second friend, Pavel Nikolaevich Medvedev, was also a regular visitor to the Bakhtins' home for meals and all those lively discussions and debates. By the time Medvedev joined the Circle, he was already more established than the others. He edited a journal and held various official academic and board appointments. He was politically active—even, briefly, mayor of Vitebsk.

The three men cared deeply for each other and were close companions. All of them were prolific, and all of them became experts at writing "under combat conditions," said Caryl Emerson, Bakhtin's chief translator into English and expert on his work and life. The state's constraints on free expression limited what words could be uttered and committed to the page, under which name, at any given time. Many of their insights were expressed in allegory, crafted carefully to conceal messages that risked triggering Soviet censorship or worse. Emerson called this era of text-making Aesopian, after the ancient children's stories. "No one speaks or writes straight," she said of Bakhtin's cohort. Every official text has "a 'more honest,' multilayered, hidden subtext that only insiders can decode."

Every text was shrouded in mystery, tinged by a measure of uncertainty as to which parts of the story reflected its author's true beliefs and interests, and which were a deflection or accommodation to a violent regime. In Bakhtin's case, these circumstances gave rise to what came to be known as an "accursed question" related to authorship that, even now, calls his legacy into question: To whom did "his" ideas belong?

The 1920s had been an especially fruitful period for the Bakhtin Circle. While the friends shared some key interests and sensibilities, they studied different disciplines, espoused diverse cultural commitments, and as time went on, found their own tactics to navigate the repression of their scholarship. It was around this time that Bakhtin's own writing shifted from its original philosophical orientation to linguistics and criticism. Scholars have argued that the change was due, at least in part, to the Soviet government's hostility to studies of ethics and aesthetics—especially any with even a whiff of religious thought. Analysis of language and literature was more likely to keep the author out of harm's way. Besides, Bakhtin was friends with linguists and critics, and naturally, they influenced one another's interests and ideas.

Voloshinov and Medvedev were working academics, but they came to be seen as lesser thinkers relative to Bakhtin, their writing perceived as lacking his depth, originality, and imagination. And so, when a handful of beautiful, philosophically sophisticated books appeared in the 1920s under their names, a life-altering process was set in motion.

It started with rumors among local scholars. And then, decades later, in the 1960s, three postgraduate students from Moscow came across Bakhtin's Dostoevsky book. By then Bakhtin was living in a small town, still exiled to utter obscurity. The students were captivated by the exquisite insights they found in his text. The author was certainly dead, they assumed, rounded up and killed as part of Stalin's "great purge," or else a casualty of the bombings in the Second World War. But with a little research, the postgrads discovered that this brilliant Bakhtin was very much alive.

A story spread that at some point during the misery and famine of the 1930s and '40s, Bakhtin had taken the only copy of a great manuscript he had been toiling over for years and, page by page, used the papers for cigarettes. "He deprived posterity of some priceless insights by tearing up one of his own manuscripts to roll his tobacco," wrote Terry Eagleton. It only added to his mystique. The students set out to salvage whatever work of Bakhtin's remained, some of it still in moldy notebooks chewed by rats in a woodshed in Saransk, a town where the Bakhtins lived in exile.

The students tracked down all of his texts they could find. Over time, scholars came across books by Voloshinov and Medvedev. When they sat down to read the volumes they'd discovered, they were surprised. Surely, they thought, prose this transcendent couldn't have been produced by those lesser writers, who by this point had died (Voloshinov of tuberculosis in 1936, Medvedev arrested and shot in 1938). With the support of other Russian academics, it was decided: Bakhtin deserved credit for Voloshinov's and Medvedev's books, too. He must have come up with the ideas, articulated the analysis, and then handed the intellectual gold to his friends, for them to publish under their own names. Fans of Bakhtin were convinced. Maybe he did it to protect himself, because his friends had more institutional cover than he did. Or maybe the giveaway was simply an extension of his radical belief that words are shared. In any case, since then, the volumes have been known as the "disputed texts."

Soon Bakhtin was enjoying a rapturous rediscovery in his own home country and abroad. A document was prepared by a Soviet agency to establish copyright. To settle the matter of the disputed texts and claim authorship of Voloshinov's and Medvedev's books once and for all, Bakhtin just had to sign a paper. He refused.

Bakhtin biographers Katerina Clark and Michael Holquist described the possible passing off of his own words and ideas as someone else's as a kind of "reverse plagiarism." The irony is rich. Bakhthin's entire body of work challenged the idea that any of us possesses our own speech. To him, a single word contains centuries and masses. Across everything he wrote, he sought traces of other people's words inflecting an individual's speech. And yet here, with the disputed texts, was a concerted attempt to attribute words to him and him alone.

> I give myself verbal shape from another's point of view,
> ultimately from the point of view of the community to
> which I belong.

Bakhtin said that. Or was it Voloshinov? Or both? Even if you check the reference list of a book that cites that line, you might not find a clear answer. The quote comes from a work called *Marxism and the Philosophy of Language*, one of the disputed texts. Often when it's cited, there's some attempt to signal uncertainty about authorship—maybe a slash between the two names, Voloshinov and Bakhtin, or a footnote.

Voloshinov-slash-Bakhtin said that when we insert other people's words into our own speech, we are producing "speech within speech, utterance within utterance, and at the same time also speech about speech, utterance about utterance." We say something using language, and at the same time about what language has the power to do.

And now I'm thinking about my own circles and the many voices that have formed this book. I can see how circles convolute simple notions of authorship, even without the political violence that hovered over the Bakhtin Circle and created conditions where, when one person said something, they all did, because association was enough to endanger each of them on the basis of what another had expressed.

The crowds that gather inside our voices create problems related to boundaries and attribution. And they create opportunities, the chance to say more than what a single person can utter alone.

Bakhtin had a metaphor for this. "I always sit on two chairs," he scrawled in one of his notebooks. "I construct my image . . . simultaneously from within myself and from the other's point of view." The authorship of this particular line, at least, is not in question. The two views he refers to, from within and without, can coexist and take concrete shape through the words contained inside a single line of speech. So yes, of course, we speak our own words and project ourselves into them. But also, we can listen within those words for the echoes and accents of others, who shape our voices and allow us, even when we are quiet, in our separate seats, to be in dialogue with others and other versions of our selves, in more than one place at a time.

Just before the holidays in 1998, Chas and I drove down to the mall in Palo Alto to take care of some shopping. I was twenty-eight years old, and we'd been together for more than four years.

"I think it's time for our parents to meet," I said, kicking my feet up onto the dashboard.

"Maybe this summer," he said.

"Hey, when they come, maybe we should surprise them and get married," I said.

This is not something I had planned to say. We had spoken many times of a future together, but the idea of a surprise wedding just kind of came to me in the moment.

"That's a great idea," he agreed.

"But how will we get them here at the same time?" I asked, because my divorced parents would never plan a simultaneous trip to San Francisco.

"We can get Jenny and Graham"—our siblings—"to help," he said.

"But who will marry us?" I asked.

We discussed the possibility of finding a cool young rabbi, but that didn't feel right because Chas isn't Jewish, and even though the Catholicism of his Irish and Italian American forebears had pretty much been extinguished by then, I didn't want there to be too much God and Hebrew. Besides, we wanted someone older who'd seen more life than we had and whose own relationship we admired, so we'd know we could believe what they said about love.

Pulling into a spot in the mall parking lot, Chas said, "I wish we knew a rabbi who was like Christine."

"Wait, what about Christine?" I said.

Yes, of course. It would be Christine, we agreed, before we even fully realized we were engaged.

We asked Christine to be our officiant and "spiritual advisor." We were kind of joking about the second part, but she took the role seriously, and her first move was to talk us out of the idea of surprising our parents.

"Lissa," she said, "wouldn't your mom want to be able to pick the outfit she'll wear to your wedding?"

I asked my friend Karen—Emily's cousin—to help me with the chuppah. She was good at chuppahs. We used fishing line to string the canopy with eighteen paper birds, a Jewish lucky number. Just as Karen had introduced me to Emily all those years ago, she was also the reason I knew Chas. In college, I'd seen him around campus and taken note of how nice he looked in a big green wool sweater he wore to parties, how when he smiled his whole face got involved, filling with folds. On Spring Weekend of my senior year, his junior, my housemates and I had people over on a Friday night, and Chas came and ate some mushrooms with a bunch of my friends. We all piled onto a bed together, sticky thighs pressing against cheeks against armpits every which way. I don't know where my boyfriend was but Karen had just broken up with hers. She and Chas laid around on the futon with the rest of us until, after a few hours, she took his hand and guided him into her room.

From then on it seemed like Chas was always at the apartment, through the last muggy weeks of school before the rest of us graduated. He showed up in the kitchen to toast a bagel and the two of us got to talking about where he'd grown up, our plans for the summer, the Faulkner thesis he was already starting to write. He wrote in a journal. I tried not to read whole sentences over his shoulder but couldn't help noticing his handwriting, boxy and all caps, a style he'd picked up from an internship at an architecture firm the summer after freshman year—an aspirational penmanship. I noticed his warmth and how easily he flowed into the conversational rhythms of our friend group. I tried not to linger on the golden skin of his lower back that showed through the gap between his T-shirt and boxers.

That summer, Chas drove out to San Francisco to be with Karen. She took him to a diner on Valencia where you could get a stack of platter-sized pancakes for five bucks, and then to Stinson Beach with her cousin Sara. But after a week or so, she broke up with him. It was a senior-year fling, she told me on the phone later. She was ready to start her real life. Chas was crestfallen, but they decided to stay friends.

After he graduated the following year, he did a summer course at the university where I was a research assistant. He called me up and we got dinner a few times. I was still with my boyfriend, so nothing romantic happened, and then Chas moved to New York. He sent me postcards now and then, telling me about the elevator shaft he lived inside of on the Lower East Side. After a couple of years, he left the East Coast for California, and around that same time, I did, too. My boyfriend dumped me the day after I arrived, which left me reeling. I ran into Chas at a party a few days later. He asked me how my boyfriend was and I said we broke up. The whole time we were talking, he stood close to me with his legs wide apart to avoid towering over me—he's about a foot taller than I am; I'm only four eleven—and I realized that no one had ever done that for me before. I found it disarmingly considerate. I called Karen to tell her I'd seen him. She said he would be very good for my heartbroken state and encouraged me to be open to whatever might happen.

Five years later, we set up the chuppah on the uneven cobblestones of our tiny garden. Christine wore a navy blue collared shirt with a pattern of little white moons and stars, wire-rimmed glasses, and thick rings on several fingers and a thumb.

For her speech, she needed to find a public language for "I love you," which was hard, given how steadfastly she and Mercy had avoided that phrase. It couldn't be corny. So she invoked one of her favorite authors, Virginia Woolf.

It was a bold move, for Christine to double-voice a wedding ceremony with a writer who, over the course of her life, had endured sexual abuse and recurring periods of debilitating depression. Sensing another was coming, one day Woolf filled the pockets of her coat with heavy stones and stepped into a river. In the note she left for her husband, she said: "What I want to say is I owe all the happiness of my life to you. . . . If anybody could have saved me it would have been you."

As part of our ceremony, Christine spoke of Woolf's interest in "the imperfections, shards of pain." Christine told us:

> There will be times of wounding and the necessity for
>   healing;
> In confidence there will be doubt,

In family there will be discord,
In conversation there will be the unspoken.
It is good to remember all that,
To be humble about the failings in others and ourselves.

At that particular moment, in the bliss and blur of a wedding day, I wasn't in the mood to think about wounds or failings—my own, Chas's, anyone's—let alone "shards of pain." Those states seemed remote at the time, someone else's burden.

And yet, when we were doing the hora, bouncing arm in arm in a circle, I watched my dad whisper something into my little brother's ear, saw my stepmother's lips tighten, my brother wince and unlink his arms, storm up the back stairs to my room. I didn't need to hear what was said to understand that he and my dad were once again roped into the knot of anger and hurt feelings that the two of them never seemed able to free themselves from for long back then. When Chas's parents smiled awkwardly through their dance to "Rocky Mountain High," I realized it was one of the only times I'd ever seen them touch each other. We knew so little about their intimacy that we'd accidentally picked the wrong John Denver song.

Christine had said in her speech that, like a spiral, marriage "swoops up the past in each of its turns toward the future." I knew what she meant when I pictured the scene as if from a helicopter hovering above us, to see what my wedding might have looked like through my dead grandparents' eyes. I felt the dotted line that connected my divorced parents and the figment forming in our collective imagination of babies we were one step closer to having because of all this. I thought of Bakhtin's faith in dialogue to carry more than other people's words into the scenes of our lives. Words are imprinted with time and defy its limits. Christine understood that we needed her to find a mix of words that would ground us in the moment and outlast it. She knew her way around a present tense that contained the past and prefigured an imperfect future. She knew that producing that specific form of time travel is in fact what weddings are for.

"Our lives are always connected to history and the making of it," she said.

She formed the scene in our backyard into a story, reminding us that the past lived inside our voices, in the memories we were making, in our bones. And with an occasion like this, she said, "a thing is made that endures."

So years later, I knew where to look when Chas and I were struggling, in our own state of discord, when the wounding Christine had talked about in the backyard was no longer a story for someone else. We found a therapist, and soon she was with us even in our most private moments, as we uttered lines that weren't exactly his or mine, and weren't exactly hers, but that we knew were necessary and that soon became part of the triangulated vocabulary of a faltering marriage.

"That sounds like 'old thinking,'" I said, parroting a phrase that the therapist sometimes used.

"I guess I'm doing that thing where I react to an exaggerated version of something you've said, so we're talking past each other," he said back, naming a habit she had noticed, using the language she provided.

It was embarrassing, but we did it anyway, every week on a couch with neither of us knowing how close to sit or whom to look at. I realized that so much of couples counseling is about learning to express someone else's speech in such a way that the other person in the relationship finally believes you're listening. For a while there, it seemed like Chas and I were never alone, always mouthing other people's words as we felt our way back to a language of our own.

We experimented with this kind of double-voicing and found it healing, even when I walked back to the car after a session and a question Bakhtin once asked scratched at my mind: "In which utterance," he wondered, "is there ever a face—and not a mask?"

There's a passage in *The Dialogic Imagination*—Bakhtin's book that Mercy inscribed for me before she and Christine moved back east—that was especially tricky to translate into English. It's where Bakhtin was working out an author's relationship to the language of a novel. The question of this relationship was fundamental to Bakhtin's thought, and its significance extended beyond the universe of literature into everyday life. A lot was riding on the word chosen by his translators, Caryl Emerson and Michael Holquist. The term they chose was "ventriloquate."

> A prose writer can distance himself from the language of his own work. . . . He can make use of language without wholly giving himself up to it, he may treat it as semi-alien or completely alien to himself, while compelling language ultimately to serve all his own intentions. The author does not speak in a given language . . . but he speaks . . . through language, a language that has somehow more or less materialized, become objectivized, that he merely ventriloquates.

In this passage, Bakhtin starts off with all the moves a prose writer can make to "people himself"—the tricks and tools at his disposal to use language that he doesn't fully possess. He presides over the narrative by operating both inside and outside of it, via the voices of his own creation. The writer stands apart from language, free to arrange and rearrange it in whatever way that serves the narrative, free to insert himself into the lines of dialogue if he wants to, or to pull back and let the words act on one another. By the end of Bakhtin's paragraph, it is clear that the author isn't in control of everything. Each time he opens his mouth, he speaks through language just as language acts through him. His entire writing voice is made up of inherited words. The language the author draws from carries a social history as long and wide as time, every word flooded with an excess of meanings that are infinitely recursive. The author makes room for other voices, other languages. He merely ventriloquates.

Notably, there is a Russian word for ventriloquate, and Bakhtin hadn't used it. A more technically precise translation of the phrase he did use was that the author speaks through language that appeared to be "at a certain distance" from the speaker's lips. So already, the translators' evocative term was a leap. And I'm grateful to them for it. "At a certain distance" leaves me cold, straining to picture a confusing image. "Ventriloquate" opens a world.

The term is rooted in the combination of two Latin words that together mean "speaking in the belly." The act of ventriloquating draws from a source that is removed from the parts of the body that form our words—the voice box, the tongue, the mouth. It's speech that emanates from deep within the gut. The ancient definition doesn't even specify whose gut, hence the mystery. Ventriloquated speech is mine and someone else's, Emily's and Jonnie's, Mercy's and Christine's, Chas's and our therapist's. The English word in Bakhtin's translated writing provides its own definition, naming and embodying the mix of voices that commingle within it and contain the movement of time.

When my father is tired, the years of suppressing his Boston accent fall away, and an "r" forms at the end of words. He says "sodar," and suddenly he's my grandfather and I'm a child again in his dining room, drinking a glass of Coke with ice. Jonnie's brother, Pete, walks through the lunch Emily held on the weekend of the memorial service, and every time he speaks or laughs, people spin around and stare. Pete's voice—"Hey, Lissy, it's good to see you"— sounds exactly like Jonnie's did. It is as if the person we've gathered to grieve suddenly stepped into the room. Mercy is teaching and says something about an Adrienne Rich poem in just the way Christine used to when they taught together, and for a moment, Christine enters the room and Mercy is speechless.

There's another ancient term that the critic David Goldblatt associates with ventriloquation: "ecstasis," which means "being beside yourself." It can be an act of dissociation, when an experience is so unbearable that you have no choice but to psychically abandon your body for the surreality of witnessing your own circumstances from a distance, fleeing and freezing at once. But being beside yourself can also be a product of feeling immensely moved, visiting the rare sense of spaciousness that opens up when you exit the boundaries of your fixed reality and see the world anew. Which is it? If I've learned anything from Bakhtin and the theories developed across all those disputed texts, I have to believe that the answer is both.

In the months after Jonnie died, Emily got a babysitter for the kids and met up with a friend at the movies. While they were settling into their seats, the friend's phone rang: her husband couldn't find their kid's favorite pajamas. "They're in the dryer, I'll be home around ten, love you," the friend said, and suddenly there was Emily, staring stiffly at the screen, newly dismayed that she'd never again have a conversation like the one her friend just had as if it were nothing. Their lives used to be similar, and now they belonged to "two separate branches of humanity," a phrase I cannot forget from Emmanuel Carrère's book *Lives Other Than My Own*, describing the feeling that divided those who did and did not lose loved ones in a tsunami that his own vacationing family had survived. For Emily, even watching a dad hoist a kid onto his shoulders felt like a knife through her heart back then, she told me, because she looked over at her own children and knew they would never again perch on the tall, sturdy tree his specific body made for theirs.

Each time Emily told me one of these stories, I made a mental note of what never to say to her or anyone else experiencing this kind of loss. Something I've learned from being close to Emily and Jonnie: how preoccupied we can become by our own actions in the face of other people's anguish. I wasn't sure how to raise the possibility of writing about Jonnie—he belonged to her—and about her grief.

Emily had her own writing to do. In one of her essays, "Widows Don't Write Thank-You Notes," she described her dreadful morning routine after Jonnie died, pulling herself out of bed alone.

> through the night's silence into the early morning bird songs and the pitter patter of children running into the bathroom and the crash of the seat cover slamming down, a wake-up call.

Later, after the empty space of a school day and getting the kids to gymnastics, through homework assignments and TV—

> we eat dinner, the three of us, in a new seating configuration, his absence screaming its presence. We eat fast to get it over with. We don't know yet how to do this . . .

I told Emily about Bakhtin, how he frees language from the dungeon of the single context, how he's always finding space for us to produce new meanings—like that little "yet" in her last line that contained the sorrow of their current situation around the dinner table and the hope that it wouldn't last forever. She liked these ideas. It was important to her that she not appear in the story only as a broken widow, full of despair.

I shared Bakhtin's quote, that our speech is filled to overflowing with other people's words, and I suggested that by showing what that looks like in actual life, *her* actual life, maybe we could honor Jonnie's voice that's still with us. We could reveal how his voice can sometimes keep hers company, even now, because words are

expansive and vital enough to make room for two. I'd been studying and writing about Bakhtin's ideas for years, I said, but watching what Emily was going through and experiencing my own loss
of Jonnie made those ideas feel new, crucial, and consoling.

Like when she talked to a medium. This was an experience we
discussed a lot. She'd connected with her first medium through a
friend in her support group for young widows, surprised that a guy
in penny loafers who worked in finance was into that kind of thing.
She was curious enough to try it, and she found the process healing. Maybe Jonnie's spirit really was out there somewhere, "watching over us." With a medium, double-voicing wasn't a literary
abstraction; it was a portal to Jonnie's presence.

Emily is a therapist. She'd listened and supported me through
endless phone calls that she never cut short, even though it couldn't
have been easy to hear me talk about difficulties in my marriage
when at least I still had one. We talked about the ways in which
Bakhtin's idea of double-voicing played out in her sessions with
couples, when she'd say something like, "I'm just going to take a
shot at this," and then express what she sensed one of them needed
to say, "that he wants more affection, more appreciation," to see
how those words might shift the energy in the room. She mostly
didn't disclose anything personal with her clients, but one guy
who'd come in to work on his marriage confessed that he'd googled her and read Jonnie's story, and she didn't know what to say
in response. Within the therapeutic dialogue, in grief groups and
printmaking and pottery workshops that she led for people who'd
lost family members, she listened for the layers within their stories,
for the presence of voices from loved ones not in the room or in the
world anymore. There was comfort in the unspoken language they
shared.

As in any other conversation with Emily, when we talked about the possibility of this book, she made encouraging sounds on the other end of the phone, asked thoughtful questions, offered new connections I hadn't been able to see. She said this, too: "I get it. You want the dead husband story."

Time passed. Over the years of living across the country from Mercy and Christine, not more than a couple of weeks went by without some kind of postcard or envelope arriving from one or both of them for one or both of us.

> Meanwhile, I had my 9th graders making valentines today and they were delightfully silly/happy to be childlike— while the senior class hit the last page of Absalom Absalom, oh my. What a tough read. I have about 4 books going, none of which knock my socks off. And, in the background, deal w/ Bad Kitty who pees here & there @ odd times (senile?) & my mom whose memory is slipping & the hum of Haiti/Iran/Obama. M&I are on serious overload w/ work @ this time of term—but try to catch a moment to crank the 𝄞 & dance in the kitchen.
> XO to everyone —
> Love,
> C

Sometimes, when Christine wrote to us about the books she assigned in class, she experimented with the author's style in her own sentences. One semester, she taught Arundhati Roy's *The God of Small Things*. Roy uses made-up words and unexpected capital letters to infuse select phrases with extra power, and Christine did the same in her letter, and then she attached a couple of essays about the book from her students. Great authors and high school sophomores wove their way through Christine's imagination in equal measure. In life, Christine was tough, unsentimental. Within books, she found a language of exuberance at just enough of a remove.

Mercy and Christine took trips to various places and came to San Francisco for long visits. We always made a big ceremony of exchanging gifts we'd picked out for each other at shops wherever we went. I paid a friend fifty bucks to buy a jacket off their back— an old-fashioned dark blue windbreaker—because the letters *MC* were embroidered on the chest.

Mercy sent us a copy of a page dedicating their school's yearbook to Christine, with a quote from Virginia Woolf—"She saw things truly"—and a line from Toni Morrison's *Beloved*: "She gather me. The pieces I am, she gather them and give them back to me in all the right order. It's good, you know, when you got a woman who is a friend of your mind."

If I can read the language of this cat, she is not telling me
she wants to die.

The Bad Kitty was sick. The Bad Kitty was Christine's cat from
before she got together with Mercy. Christine was beside herself.

I don't see it in her steady walk to the grass she will claw,
to the end of the front walk where she sits and stares—in
her quick feet when I toss Mr. Mouse or her staring @ my
piece of chicken. I look at her and say—what? "I'm going
to 'kill you' in 3 days? I'm going to 'let you go' before you
are miserable? I'm going to 'spare you' the pain of . . ." I'm
sorry, but . . . What are the words for this?

Bad Kitty was put down by a compassionate vet on a Tuesday in
June. This was 2010, a decade after Christine married Chas and
me. Something shifted. Maybe it had already shifted, but this is
when I started to really notice. Christine was overwhelmed by grief.
Every night for months, she lit the wick of a lantern, left it on the
red table not far from Bad Kitty's grave in the yard, and said, again
and again, "The light is still on for you."

Mercy called to tell me how rigidly ritualized and closed off Christine was becoming. She'd told Christine that she was worried about her despondency, encouraged her to see a therapist, had an old friend with expertise in animal grief come for a weekend to see if she could get through to her, but nothing seemed to help. I noticed it, too, when they visited us and Christine insisted that we only go to restaurants we'd been to before. She seemed a little checked out, slow to laugh or respond to the particulars of our conversations but then strangely fixated on faraway global news like the crisis in Iran. Mostly she just wanted to read the paper or sit quietly in the other room and look at a book while we cooked.

At one point Mercy and I were alone doing an exercise routine from a DVD. It cracked me up to watch her, a lifelong jock whose job had her pacing the sidelines of an athletic field every afternoon, here in my bedroom doing goofy Tae Bo moves in the narrow space between my bureau and nightstand. During the cooldown, she told me that she was frustrated Christine never wanted to go to the gym anymore. Mercy's always been obsessive about sports, so I didn't give it much thought.

"She's not really interested in sex," Mercy said, her legs extended in front of her, folding forward from her hips and reaching for her toes. That didn't sound great. Christine had been acting off lately, but I wasn't overly worried. I figured the downside of their big age gap was finally showing up, like Mercy's parents had predicted. I had never believed it would make a difference. I pointed to the two of them with their matching spiky haircuts and scuffed boots and said, "See? Look at them!" With their kitchen blackboard for daily notes, the passages from student essays read out loud to each other while grading papers every night. "Look how beautiful it is for them," I used to say when people doubted they'd make it, even though, when Christine rode from New Hampshire to San Francisco on the back of a motorcycle in the early '70s, Mercy had just been born. Maybe I'd been naive not to realize that at some point, their age gap would become an issue.

They took a trip to Paris. Christine was so sullen and inward that after a couple of days, Mercy turned to her in the hotel bed and asked, "Where have you gone?"

Mercy fell for someone else. A man. She waited a little bit, thinking it might not amount to more than flirtation. But once she realized she was about to act on her feelings, she told Christine. She told me, too. She went on about how thoughtful and funny he was. How present. I didn't want to hear it. I hated to imagine her laughing with him, writing to him. I hated this for Christine but also for the four of us. It felt like something precious to me was breaking, the sense that it was special and ours alone.

That Thanksgiving, I kept leaving the table at my aunt and uncle's house to find an empty bedroom where I could talk to Mercy, and then Chas was on with Christine, and then Christine called me, and later in the hotel bathroom, Chas and I brushed our teeth and tried to make sense of everything.

"I can't believe this is really happening."

"Do you think this is actually it, like it's over between them?"

"Christine sounded awful."

"They have to sit through department meetings together. How's that gonna work?"

"They're still sleeping in the same bed."

"Ugh, I feel sick."

"It's all so fucking sad."

What must it be like, to be left? Chas and I couldn't stop talking about it. And then there were the things we didn't talk about. Things having to do with the reckless freedom of turning away from the life you have, wanting more. For a whole different future to open up before you, a different person to create it with.

And yet still, I hoped maybe this was something Mercy had to go through, and then she and Christine would heal and come back together again. And even if that didn't happen, I thought it was possible that we could find our way to some bittersweet rearrangement. I thought of my own parents. When I was three or four, my father left my mother for another woman. When he introduced me to her, I let her push me on a swing at a playground, and it didn't take long to allow myself to love her. My mom and dad sometimes spoke about their time together with tenderness. "Look what we got out of it," they said, gesturing toward my sister and me.

I thought of a story Mercy told at our wedding. We had asked her to be in charge of the cake. She covered it in white fondant and then cut out red letters to spell sentences across the frosting, arranging lines from Christine's speech and a Virginia Woolf quote so the words began and ended off the cake, leaving only fragments of the quotations intact. Out of spools, plumbing supplies, and wire, Mercy made two chess pieces and sat them side by side in the middle of the cake to represent the bride and groom.

When she presented the cakes, she made a toast about how entering a relationship was like dropping into a chess game that was already in play. She likened that experience to how she thought about reading. To experience the characters and scenes in a novel, the moments and meanings, she said, you had to allow yourself to be swept into a story that was underway by the time you got there.

You had to accept that the narrative started before you and would go on beyond you, that it was never all yours.

This memory helped me imagine that maybe our intertwined lives were a more complicated story than I'd thought. Maybe it wouldn't all work out with the four of us, growing old together, reconnecting over the years in the headquarters of our friendship. But maybe it could still be a good, long story that held us all.

I had a certain kind of story in my mind about Bakhtin, too. When I was in grad school and first learned about the disputed texts, the idea that Bakhtin surrendered his brilliant writing to two lesser scholars made me love him even more. It seemed that he was so divested from the idea that we possess our own speech, he shrugged off credit for what was rightfully his. The move matched his dialogic theory. If meaning is a product of more than one person, texts are always shared, Bakhtin believed. "Creativity," he wrote, "is in essence anonymous."

And yet, the disputed texts were never anonymous. Actual people came up with the ideas, wrote the words, made money from the sales, built reputations off the influence, got their names on the book jackets. And others didn't. While freeing words from the "dungeon of a single context," ventriloquation can also damage the lives of people whose own words get subsumed into the speech of others. The issue was not that no one got credit for the creativity within the disputed texts. The accursed question is whether it was the right or wrong people who did.

There was one person for whom this question was acutely personal. When Medvedev—the most established of the young intellectuals in the Bakhtin Circle, certainly the only one with the clout to rally needed support after Bakhtin's arrest—was shot dead in 1938, he left behind a son.

"I knew him quite well," Professor Craig Brandist told me when I called him up in 2018. Craig runs the Bakhtin Centre at the University of Sheffield in the UK. I asked about Medvedev's son, Yuri. They saw each other often, Craig said, in St. Petersburg, Britain, Finland: various places around Europe where scholars met to discuss the legacy of Bakhtin's thought. The two men rode an overnight train together to a conference once back in 2000. Yuri was ailing by then, having recovered from a heart attack and retired from his work rehabilitating victims of Stalin's purges and later editing films. Post-retirement, he dedicated himself to rehabilitating the reputation of his father, who was killed when Yuri was eighteen months old.

"He was a very warm man, a principled man," Craig said of Yuri. "He was offended by the way his father had been treated, by the people who controlled Bakhtin's estate, and especially his manuscripts. Especially the fact that the English translation of Medvedev's work *The Formal Method* was published in the American translation in Bakhtin's name. He was very angry about that."

"What significance does all this have—authorship, a name?" Bakhtin asked.

Profound significance, if you're Yuri Medvedev.

As a practical matter, Yuri's mother was alive when *The Formal Method* was published in the US. Royalties from that translation went to Bakhtin's estate, Craig told me. "His mother got nothing." But this was not only a practical matter. This was a son who felt his father had been written out of history, "treated as a ventriloquist's dummy," is how Craig put it, reduced to a mere mouthpiece for another man's brilliance.

When Yuri went to Bakhtin conferences to present papers aimed at establishing his father's authorship of the works later attributed to Bakhtin, the Russian academics who most passionately credited Bakhtin for those texts refused to attend Yuri's sessions, Craig told me.

The way Yuri saw it, he'd lost his father to state-sponsored terror before his second birthday, and then, decades later, was denied his father's proper legacy. It was the opposite of what had happened to Bakhtin. Consider, for example, the story of that manuscript whose pages Bakhtin allegedly incinerated during wartime, using the paper to roll his tobacco. We know now that the more likely reason that book was never published is because Bakhtin never finished it, that he had only gotten as far as rough drafts of chapters scrawled in notebooks. Bakhtin was acknowledged for books he'd never written; his friend Medvedev was denied full credit for the ones he had. As far as Yuri was concerned, his father's accomplishments had been erased, so he clung to any piece of his father's voice that survived.

Yuri had two prized possessions. One was a photo of his father, holding a tiny Yuri on his shoulders. The other was a metal nameplate that had been nailed to his father's door. The plate was engraved with two names: Pavel Nikolaevich Medvedev, the father, and underneath it, Yuri, the son. Taken together, these two objects were a kind of evidence, of how much he mattered to his father, of his father's actual presence in the world.

Yuri is gone now. He died before he finished the two-volume set of his father's writings that he'd been working so hard to compile. But Bakhtin would remind us that there is no such thing as a last word. Every dialogue will at some point be given new life.

E mily has a folder on her laptop filled with files from Jonnie's devices: videos, audio recordings, text messages. She told me the texts had posed the biggest challenge. She'd spent hours at the Apple Store. The guy said he'd need to use a special program to extract them, which he was only willing to do after Emily told him that her husband had just died and she would need access to those texts for the rest of her life.

In that same folder, Emily saved the voicemails she'd pulled from her own phone after Jonnie died. She played them for me, one after the other.

Hey Sugar, it's me, just calling to check on how you're doing, which I hope is okay. Call me when you get a chance. Bye.

Hey sorry about that, I was just getting Maxine out of the bath, call me back, okay bye.

"Oh my God," I said at the sound of his voice, which I had always loved, the smile you could hear in the shape of his words, the sudden boom of his outrageous laugh.

Hello! Give me a call! Call me back, bye!

Hey Sugar, it's me. Just calling to check in with you, give me a call when you get a chance, bye.

Hey Sugar, it's me. I hope you're having—I hope your trip is okay. I love you and I'll see you. I love you. Give me a call when you get a chance.

This last one was sleepy, maybe a drink or two in. He traveled a lot for work, and I pictured him lying in a hotel bed, wishing Emily were there.

Hey Sugar, it's me. Just calling to check in on you, give me a call when you get a chance, I'll be in meetings most of the day but I'll try and reach you when I get a break. Okay bye.

Hey Sugar, just calling you back. Call me back when you can. Okay bye.

Hey Sugar it's me just calling to make sure you survived. Give me a call when you get a chance. Okay bye.

Hey Sugar, it's me, I'm just calling to check in on you. I got a little bit of sleep. I love you.

Sorry I'm not there.

I saw a reading once by the writer Cord Jefferson called "Leave a Message," which starts off like a trend piece about why millennials hate voicemail. Like so many of us, Jefferson found the technology supremely annoying and admitted to speeding through the long, rambling messages his mom left on his phone, barely listening and wishing she'd just get to the point. Then she was diagnosed with breast cancer. After visiting her in hospice when he knew she'd die soon, he had dinner with a friend who'd lost his own parent to suicide. "Do you have any recordings of her voice?" the friend asked. He told Jefferson a single message from his father was more important to him than anything else his dad had left behind.

That got Jefferson thinking about the power of a loved one's voice and what we lose if we abandon technologies that save it for us. He cited neuroscience research showing that hearing your mother's voice has pretty much the same effect on the brain as hugging her. When Jefferson wants to hear his mom now that she's gone, he's left only with a one-minute message in which she thinks out loud about which housing option makes the most sense for an upcoming visit to see him—whether she should go with a hotel or Airbnb. It's entirely mundane. And yet, this recording is, he says now, "the only possession I have that I really care about."

Each of Jonnie's messages was a dialogue, containing his voice from before, when he didn't know what would happen to him or that he had so little time left, and the Jonnie of now, a presence that stretches beyond his death. Listening to the recordings, I let myself imagine that Jonnie really was still checking on Emily, making sure she was okay, calling her Sugar. His voice spoke simultaneously from the time before and after he died.

Again and again, Emily played the messages and watched the videos in her folder, except when she was too raw and knew that the sound of his voice would unravel her. It was a practice of remembering, or more specifically, not forgetting. She listened and heard different meanings in his lines—*calling to make sure you survived, sorry I'm not there.* She listened out of a fear of letting go—"that all of the sudden, it wouldn't mean as much, that the importance of him wouldn't feel as tangible, if I didn't keep watching."

The avant-garde artist Laurie Anderson and her husband, Lou Reed of the Velvet Underground, had been inseparable for decades when Reed was diagnosed with hepatitis and then liver cancer. In his final moments, at their home on Long Island, Anderson held him in her arms and talked to him. "I have never seen an expression as full of wonder as Lou's as he died," she wrote after it was over. "His heart stopped. He wasn't afraid. I had gotten to walk with him to the end of the world . . . And death? I believe that the purpose of death is the release of love."

Seven years after Reed died, Anderson became an artist-in-residence at a university in Australia. She collaborated with some scientists there who were working on artificial intelligence projects that combined technology and creative expression. They had developed a system that scoured the internet for every word Anderson had ever expressed—in interviews, writing, verses, songs—and fed that corpus into a program that wrote poems in her voice. It did the same for Lou Reed. And then, mind-bendingly, the scientists asked the program to combine their two voices into one, like an impossible larynx capable of generating the words of two artists who adored each other, one alive, the other who had already walked past the end of his world.

Anderson told the *New York Times* that plenty of the poetry produced by the AI was nonsense, or just boring. But some of it felt like magic. "Sometimes she sits there with the hunger of an addict," Sam Anderson wrote in the *Times,* "feeding words and pictures into the engine, seeing what comes out." For years after he died, she saved the texts. But after a while, "she realized that the texts were infinite. She could have one whenever she needed it. So she read them and then let them go."

Anderson's gesture, the reading and releasing of those synthesized lines, echoes how the scholar Irina Sandomirskaia describes Bakhtin's understanding of love: "an almost imperceptible caress that at the same time is a farewell; a desire that relinquishes all power and possession; a longing that lets go."

Mercy and Christine moved out of the house they shared in 2011. When Christine packed up her belongings, she put aside two boxes that she labeled "for M when I'm gone" and mailed to us the objects that reminded her too much of Mercy to keep or toss. A leather bag they bought in Italy. An old enamel stapler. Small tin ashtrays from different places where they'd traveled. And she left poems and notes on Mercy's porch and under her windshield wipers. Once Christine spotted one of her own letters, unopened, on the seat of Mercy's truck and then wrote her another letter about that experience, "with all its mess of orange peels and gum wrappers and coffee cups and the address where he works on the dashboard, my gesture sits like another piece of trash. You threw so much away."

Christine smashed framed love letters and photos Mercy had given her over the years, and, in her sixties, did something she hadn't since she was a queer and closeted teenager: cut herself with the broken glass. "Adrift in the howling," she wrote in a poem— one of many she'd butterfly-clipped in a manila envelope and sent to me—"anger held the sharp edge of whatever I could find and slashed my right hand, my left arm again and on another night, again . . ."

She wrote to Chas that she felt both old and too young to be without love, and that she didn't have the imagination to believe love might be possible for her again. If it were, Christine wrote, "I still wish it could be w/ her."

Christine spent the next academic year guest-teaching at a different school to get some distance from the situation. When she came back, it was summertime, and Chas and I were heading to a place his parents had rented on the south coast of Massachusetts. By now Mercy's relationship with the guy had started to crumble. She and Christine had seen each other a few times, even shared a smoke now and then. We knew it was probably a bad idea but decided anyway to invite them, both of them, to meet up with us at the beach. We thought maybe enough time had passed.

A lot of the visit felt pretty normal. I led a yoga class on a deck over the sand. We floated in the water. Mercy prepared a feast for dinner.

After we ate, we sat on the sun-bleached rug in the living room, drinking gin and tonics, and Christine began rubbing Mercy's shoulders and back. Mercy's body always hurt, from all the sports she'd played, injuries that never fully healed, stress, and inheritance. I watched her lean into the pressure, angle her neck as if to make more room for the feeling of release. She let Christine's hands move her gently, back and forth. She closed her eyes.

Christine held her face still, expressionless. She hadn't said too much the whole day and evening; she seemed absent in a way I thought at the time had to do with her hurt. But I could see what she longed for, how she was willing it to be so—that the touching would lead to something more, that they'd go to bed that night with warmth between them, with heat, that they'd wake up close again, that the reconnection would last. I knew it would be complicated, probably reckless, but I wanted that for them, too. For them and for us.

It was time to do the dishes, and Mercy joined me at the sink. I grabbed a towel for drying, and with soapy hands, in a quiet voice, she told me that she was planning to call the man she'd been seeing even though he'd said they were through. She wanted an explanation. At least he owed her that. Didn't he owe her that? I didn't know what he owed her. All I knew was this: Mercy was not coming back to Christine.

Christine moved to Ogunquit, Maine, to a cottage her mom left empty when she moved to a nursing home. If she kept living in the town where she'd been with Mercy, she'd face the daily realizations of all that she had lost. She'd keep running into Mercy at the grocery store or along the paths on campus, and she'd be hit, again and again, by the cold distance between them. Besides, there was something very Christine about piling what was left of her belongings into her orange VW bug and driving north to live alone, commuting to school in New Hampshire to teach and coach. She leaned into the hard edges of her mother's barely insulated rooms.

Before the move, Christine made a stack of everything Mercy had ever created for her over all their years together—the letters, poems, drawings, and block prints—and lit the whole thing on fire. "It took a long time, more than an hour," she wrote later about what she'd done, in a letter addressed to Mercy that she sent to both of us. "There must have been over 1000 pages in those boxes I will not carry with me."

That last line was a reference to *The Things They Carried*, a book by Tim O'Brien about the possessions soldiers bring with them into war. I know this because Christine cited O'Brien a lot.

She and Mercy both taught his book in their lit classes at school, and he was one of the first writers Chas bonded with them about.

I pulled the book off the shelf after I got Christine's letter and reread some passages.

> The thing about a story is that you dream it as you tell it, hoping that others might then dream along with you, and in this way memory and imagination and language combine to make spirits in the head.

That's often what it felt like, being with Christine around this time. Like she was dreaming. She was walking around with spirits in her head, scenes of herself and Mercy as they had been, and she was mistaking those imagined dialogues for reality.

O'Brien said stories can "revive, at least briefly, that which is absolute and unchanging." In a story, O'Brien boasted, "I can steal her soul." I'm pretty sure Christine would never have thought of it the way O'Brien did—that her attempts to get Mercy back had anything to do with stealing. But that's what it looked like to me. And anyway, by this time, I knew her letters wouldn't work. Mercy had mostly stopped reading them. There were too many. They were too intense. I sensed Christine knew this was the case, which was why she also sent the letters to me.

"And I don't know which was the saddest thing," Christine went on to write in that same letter about torching Mercy's words, "watching your penmanship turn to ash . . . or ripping pages I had believed in. The heat of the fire made me sweat in my flannel shirt and I had to put some things in the Blue Recycling Bin b/c they wouldn't burn."

In a different letter, this one addressed to me, Christine wrote to tell me how hurtful it was that Mercy "didn't even TRY. She didn't say, 'Christine, we need some help, we need to work on some things because I'm unhappy.'" I imagined Christine typing out the exact words she longed to hear, projecting herself into the first-person who'd left her. At least here on the page, she was still entitled to a "we" they could inhabit together. She could nest Mercy's wished-for words within her own. And yet, shattered and furious as she was, Christine still worried for Mercy, cared for her.

> Chaser just called. I love him. I can't write anymore and
> have maybe said too much b/c you NEED TO BE THERE
> FOR HER, she needs you so so so much.

In the poem Mercy wrote for Christine's birthday when they spent their year in San Francisco, she asked, "If we could not write, would the contour of our legs entwined together be parentheses or a slash?" The answer turned out to be a slash, but not the kind she had in mind when she wrote the poem. Parentheses would have put brackets around their hard times, set them off as a difficult period in a long relationship, a painful aside they could look back on afterwards and think, *That was close*. But they got a slash instead. A mark that looks like a blade and a wound, a red diagonal line on the pale soft flesh of Christine's inner arm that brought her a small, temporary, and inadequate sense of relief.

And yet, even after she lit the papers on fire, still, Christine wrote. Some things, after all, wouldn't burn. Staring at the flames, Christine didn't know which was the saddest thing, tearing Mercy's pages into pieces or watching her loopy handwriting go up in smoke. For me, when I read the letter Christine wrote to Mercy about the fire, I didn't have to ask myself what was the saddest thing. In my mind, it was a single line, all by itself, at the center of the page, an unrequited question:

What, for example, did you do all day?

Because that's what we lose when we are left. Knowing what they had for lunch, whether they remembered to call a nephew for his birthday, if they had time to throw in a load of laundry. We are no longer entitled to this information, in all its banal and exquisite intimacy. Suddenly it is unseemly even to want to know, and yet we can't help it. So now we are both alone and chastened.

> Language does not confuse me, silence does. Yours, every day, every night now. You, talking on the phone with any-one but me, shaping meaning I am not meant to hear.
> I have nothing to read.

When she found out about the fire, Mercy was devastated, worse than any other moment in the breakup. "We were two people who valued our writing between each other more than anything, it's where we found a shape for things that life could never have given us. She was erasing me, and choosing to," Mercy said. I sensed her heart closing. She had a lot of shame for what she had done to Christine, how she had left her. She couldn't forgive herself. But with her own letters burned, she couldn't forgive Christine either.

In the absence of Mercy's words, the boundaries around Christine gave way. Christine had lost what Bakhtin would have called her "verbal shape," the contour formed through the words we share with others, by what the people in our lives see and say through us.

With nothing of Mercy's to read, Christine couldn't shore herself up within an outline that would hold.

"A word is a bridge thrown between myself and another," said the Bakhtin Circle. But a bridge isn't a bridge if the ground on one side is eroding, and on the other side, the land is gone. It's a relic of an impossible connection, a ruin. The word hangs in the air.

In 2013, Christine started seeing a therapist named Andy, who listened patiently and told her she had carried Mercy for so long, she needed to put her down and move on. He recommended an antidepressant. "I looked it up on Mr. Google," said Christine.

Aside from the occasional web search, she avoided whatever modern technology she could. She wrote letters in longhand, put off getting a cell phone, refused to set up voicemail on the landline. But in time she relented on email and hit up the nice lady in tech support at school to help her create her first account. Soon, her messages to Chas and me picked up in frequency, and so did her use of exclamation points and stray punctuation. I knew this wasn't normal, but I still thought it was heartbreak. Or maybe she was writing to us drunk?

June 2013

Chaser,
I went to the beach today . . . Too damn cold
to go in!!!. . . . so I took some strokes in the
River, which was warmish. . . .
    & I'm loving Edwide Danticat . . . have
read ALL her books!!! (about memory . . .

& family & myths. . .) I think you would
love her novels. . . .

Tomorrow I will go to the theater in town
to see some shorts from the PINK film festival
(gay!) I hope there won't be Lesbian ones. . . .
I've written many love poems about MC. . . .
I keep hoping . . . she will see the errors of
her ways . . . & come back to me. . . .
Love
C

Christiner,
I found one of the Danticats you
recommended, but I'm holding out for hard
cover. Simone and I are reading Old Man
and the Sea. I thought it might be hard,
so little dialogue, so much sadness etc.
But she's very into it.
I hadn't read it since 8th grade. I love how
he talks to the fish and periodically says,
"I wish the boy were here."
xoxox
C

Chas
Glad you cried @ the end of OLD MAN &
THE SEA!!! With Simone..

Don't think I can come to SF. . . . M&I
lived there together. . . . & I'm still in love w/
her. . . . wrote a # of "love poems" about/to
her. . . There are 2 boxes of stuff for her
when I dead & gone. . . . and you know,
don't you?, that I want some of my ashes

into the Pacific??? Maybe Lissa told you
that. . . . she said, "It was an honor" &
M. said that, too. . . . I'm not planning on
exiting any time soon!!!
Love
C

All through spring and summer that year, Christine wrote to Chas and me about what she was reading, whether she'd made it to the ocean or gym that day, maybe a bit of political news, but she ended most sentences in ellipses, as if she couldn't be bothered to finish her thoughts until they took her back to Mercy, a constant, painful, irresistible absence. Chas forwarded one of her emails to me with the line, "Doesn't seem like it's letting up one bit." Her letters sat unopened for days. I wrote to Chas: "OMG I don't think I can take much more of this." She sent Chas notes detailing her sexual longing for Mercy, and it got so out of hand that Chas asked for my advice on how to tell Christine that maybe she didn't have to share quite as much with him about that stuff. Christine never used to speak openly of sex except when she talked about politics or cited passages from books. We had a running joke that she was incapable of saying the word "vagina" out loud. Chas sensed that her graphic emails weren't a product of a boldness she'd previously suppressed. He sensed there was something else going on, but he didn't understand what.

The last time we had her up to Chas's parents' place in Massachusetts, my mother-in-law asked Christine about a recent trip. "I don't know how to answer that question," Christine snapped with obvious impatience, and then she turned and walked away.

Christine had always been reserved, but this was different. She was acting like she didn't want to be there and yet wouldn't leave. When anyone tried to talk to her, she barely made eye contact and didn't ask anything back. Even the way she moved was off. When she pushed through the screen door and headed for the bike she was borrowing from Chas's dad, she looked straight ahead and didn't check to see if the rest of us were ready, almost like she had to block out whatever was in her peripheral vision to get where she was going. My mother-in-law wasn't pleased, and we had to find an excuse not to invite her back.

"You are a feminist and you are harassing Mercy," their very close friend Jamie from the school's religious studies department told her. "If she were to report what's happening to the school, you would be charged. It must end."

"I don't know if I can stop," Christine said.

This was classic Christine—to wrap a surrender inside a refusal. It was the best she could offer and maybe the first time she admitted how little control she had over her own mind and actions.

Sometimes I blamed her therapist, Andy.

"What's with Andy? Can't he make her stop?" I said to Chas after hanging up on yet another circular conversation with Christine. I can see now that Andy couldn't make her stop. We couldn't make her stop. And Christine definitely wouldn't, couldn't stop herself.

July 2013

Christiner,
We are going to Nonquitt, but I'm
in the doghouse with my mother for
not carving out more family time,
so I'm not allowed to invite guests!
Any chance I could lure you to Boston
for dinner on Sat Aug 10?
Xoxox
C

Chaser
I will bring ELECTRIC MICHELANGELO
to Boston & give it to you (paperback!)
   I just found out that both Leonardo &
Michelangelo were GAY!!! (although that
word wasn't around in the 15th century). . . .
Which explains why M. made so many male
nudes. . . .!!!!
   Rained all day here. . . . I walked down to
the beach in my slicker & cap. . . . the water
was rough & warm. . . .
   Haven't heard anything from M. about
why she's not coaching this fall!!! My

therapist will be relieved. . . . but she asked
me to coach w/ her, so I am confused!!!! I
was hoping to win her back on the
sidelines!!!!
Love
C

> Christiner
> I need a dip in the ocean! I think I'll save it
> for the east coast. I'm off to a business
> dinner and Lissy will be having dinner with
> Emily, who's in town for a few days.
> She's having a rough time.
> oxoxxo
> C

Chaser
Andy still thinks, at age 64, that I need to
"move on." I know he thinks that & we
smile @ one another. . . . He notices a
pause . . . "what's my life w/out Mercy?"
She was the love of my life, Chas; I can't
abandon Hope. . .
Love
C

> Christiner,
> I know how much you love Mercy, and I don't
> expect that will ever go away. But I do worry
> that you're hurting yourself by hoping so
> hard that you will return to being lovers. I
> don't think you guys will ever get back
> together in the way you were before. I hope,
> though, that you guys can find a way back to

a new kind of friendship, so you won't be
living your life without Mercy. It hurts me to
say that so bluntly; I loved you two as a
couple. But I think it needs saying. I love you
and I love Mercy, but I think it's hurting your
friendship with her to hope and expect you'll
return to the way it was—and it would be
even worse if you guys stopped being friends.
I'm so sorry for the harsh words. It's because
I love you and I want to be honest with you.

xoxoxoxo

Love,

Chas

Chaser,

Thanks for being honest. . . .and I know I
am "hurting myself" with my hopes . . . but I
can't help it. . . . And I know you loved us
"as a couple." I did, too!!! I haven't heard
from her in AGES. . . . she says she wants
friendship; but, doesn't follow through.

I want you to know that I am taking
generic Lexapro for depression. . . . it makes
me feel calmer. . . . although I have written 2
more poems. . . . about loving her. . . .
drawing the acorns I walk by on my way to
the beach. . . . there were acorns under the
tree where we first kissed. . . . by the tidal
river, under a full moon. . . . so when I see a
full moon I get sad. . . .

My therapist wants me to go to THE
FRONT PORCH. . . . Lesbian bar. I
think they may be only couples . . . he says
that my fear. . . . Jamie also wants me to go,

too. . . . maybe next week end???? We mostly
talked politics. . . . left M on the
sidelines. . . . It was nice not to discuss
her. . . .

How are you???? I thought Roma dived off
the high board!!! Can I see a picture of
that????
Love
C

We stopped in Boston on our way home to San Francisco from Chas's parents' house. The plan was for Chas and Christine to meet up for dinner, and I would bow out and stay in Cambridge with Emily. It hadn't yet been a year since Jonnie died. We explained to Christine that I would have to miss her this time.

I'd grown tired of Christine's fixation on getting back together with Mercy. I was talking to Mercy nearly every day, so I was getting a lot of details on Christine's relentless pursuit of her, and like Jamie, I was alarmed. It felt like harassment. It had to stop. My interactions with Christine felt blunt, reduced. I loved her and didn't want to hurt her feelings, but I thought she'd understand and was glad she and Chas would have some time to connect.

The doorbell rang when I was already in my pajamas on the second floor of Emily's house. Christine presented herself, unsmiling, in the doorway of the kids' room where I was spending the night. I was taken aback. Christine would normally be mindful not to impose herself, knowing the situation. She would be considerate of Emily's need for privacy, her palpable grief. Instead, Christine barged into Max's room, jeans hanging off her shrunken frame, exuding impatience. I rushed to get dressed and get her out the door.

After she left, Emily turned to me. "Liss," she said, "there's something wrong with your friend."

"I know, I'm sorry, that was weird," I said, feeling bad that we'd intruded on her evening. "She's not usually like that."

"No," Emily said. "That's not what I'm talking about."

Emily had watched illness come over her parents. She'd seen her dad—usually so put together—with the messy hair and untucked shirts of someone who'd lost track of vanity. As a therapist, she knew the importance of naming a thing that was wrong. With all she'd gone through, she didn't have a lot of patience for talking around what no one else was willing to see or say.

"There's something really off," Emily said. "She's not all there."

I was almost—almost—ready to hear her.

August 2013

Christiner—
Thanks for trekking down to Boston
yesterday. It was great to see you.
You get back to Ogonquitt ok?
Talk soon.
Xoxox
Chas

Chaser
Great to see you, too!!! And Lissa &
Emily. . . . & Simone w/ that front tooth
missing!!!! Thanks for the ride to mr parking
lot!!!
    Got home @ 11. . . . Had a little trouble
getting back onto Tobin Bridge. . . . but
made it. . . . . passed the Dunks where
M & I decided to tell Peter about us. . . . .
read a chapter then went to bed & woke
up @ 9. . . .
    Did the speed boat guy get arrested????
Love
C

No, it was an accident. I don't think
there are any criminal charges.

David called & he will come up next week,
when I have meetings @ school!!!!
Love
C

School meetings? Anything I should
worry about there??
xoxox
C

Nope!!! Dept mtg @ 8:30, so I will have to
get up early for that!!!! Mercy doesn't feel
like she will be welcome. . . . She's not
coaching. . . . You might send her a card of
support???? Her hair is LONG!!! . . . . I hope
she gets it cut. . . . she doesn't look like
herself. . . . & she has her toenails painted!!!!
Love
C

Mercy with long hair? I can't imagine it!
xoxo
C

Chaser
Found a book for $4.98: STONES FROM
THE RIVER, by Ursula Hegi. . . . I liked her
other one. . . . so I bought it!!!
Stare @ Mercy a lot. . . . her hair is very
curly in the back!!!

Cold, gray & foggy when I got home; so, I
walked to the beach to get my face wet. . . .
& bought a new bathing suit for $63 fucking
dollars!!!! It's Black!!!
Love
C

F all came. Mercy and Christine would run into each other at school. Mercy told me about one time, when they were at an evening event. Christine came in for a hug and stared at Mercy the whole time, followed her around the room, close enough for Mercy to smell her mix of sweat and detergent. I wondered if Christine felt Mercy recoil, even if she didn't let it stop her. I thought about the visceral effects of curdled love.

Christine resumed her role as the assistant crew coach. One afternoon, she was out with a group of freshmen by a river near campus. Christine had them climb into a shell and pushed them out onto the water. Then she got into her car and drove off, went home. No explanation. This was baffling and a major school policy violation. The fallout was inevitable. A senior administrator called a meeting and told Christine to bring a friend. She chose Jamie. "We're really concerned. We're worried about you," the dean and department head told Christine, and they ticked through a list of strange behaviors that were totally unlike her. They wanted Christine to see a doctor. Maybe it was a health issue. Maybe she was depressed. At first, Christine resisted, dismissed the meeting as a scolding. But then, there was a second incident of her leaving kids unattended. Jamie told me that

that's when the school drew the line and put her on administrative leave, which would only cover her for so long. If she wanted the leave to be reclassified as medical, she absolutely needed to be assessed.

Chaser
Good session w/ Andy today. . . . he called an
Assement guy & will get back to me!!!
About the date for the appointment.

I said I didn't think M would come back
to me: she has her whole life ahead of her;
why would she return to a 64 year old
woman???? I also said I fantasize about M&I
making love. . . . he said I should try dating
other women!!! He always says that!!!

Hope all is well in SF!!!!
Love
C

Assessment for what?
Dating other women wouldn't be
the end of the world, would it?
If it doesn't go well, you can ditch out
early & get back to a good book!
oxoxox
C

Chaser
Jamie & therapist think I should go on Med
Leave. . . . while all the testing happens. . . . .
I'm kinda scared of that. . . . what if
something is really wrong w/ my Brain???
Love
C

Christiner,
I sure hope there's nothing wrong with
your brain, but I'm glad you're getting it
checked out. I'm betting it's just the games
that grief can play on a person. Maybe they
can also look for side effects from the meds
you are taking. I've known people who
(with help from doctor) need to play with
the dosage to get it exactly right.
I'll call soon.
Xoxoxo
C

Finally, on October 9, 2013, Christine went in for an assessment of her cognitive functioning. It was Chas's birthday. He joked in an email that she'd picked an auspicious day and wished her luck. She hoped they'd give her smoke breaks between tests and worried that her poor sleep the night before might hamper her performance.

October 2013

Chaser & Lissa

It was kinda frustrating. . . . . lots of math & spell-ing. . . . . . Then @ the end a Card Game w/ 4 cards on the top row. . . . I thought it was matched by color; but, I was wrong. . . . . then I thought it was by the #s on the card; I was wrong again!!!!

He read off some numbers & had to repeat them. . . . I did OK w/ that. . . . . Then he read some nouns. . . . . . toooooo many; & I forgot some. . . . . I hope that doesn't affect my "score."

He's a small man with wild hair & pants low on his hips & a frayed sweater vest. . . . . but he was kind & gentle & said some of the tests were Really Hard. . . .

Will go next Wed. for a follow up. . . . He did grant me a smoke break!!!!

I went to Golden Egg for a grilled cheese . . . he said I could eat it in the Conf. Room where I had my Assessment. . . .

So that's that. . . . . Andy recommended a Cat Scan. . . . . oh dear. . . . .

Love,

C

The CAT scan came back normal, which ruled out some scary scenarios, but not all. The diagnosis from all the other assessments was both wretched and obvious.

> MRI showed some white spots (chronic smoking!!!) and brain Atrophy. . . . He said my intelligence might ward off memory loss. . . . . I have sooooo many memories of M&I together!!!!! Did I tell you that already????

Cognitive decline.

> Got in today!!!! It's always good for my self-esteem to get into the SEA.

The doctor gave her some medication, and Jamie found an organization that supports people with memory loss, to get their help figuring out next steps.

> I found the one I wanted, rising & rising & caught it before it tumbled into foam. . . . . . Sox lost last night. . . . . let's see what they do tonight!!!!

I'm ashamed that it took so long for Chas and me to realize that what we were seeing in all those emails, the disregard for social cues, those affectless phone conversations and endless repetitions, the state of her hair and clothes; it wasn't just heartbreak. Yes, she was full of sadness and resentment over Mercy's betrayal.

> Long email from M . . . she seems worried about me, which is a good thing!!!!

But the obsessiveness, the sentence fragments, the time Mercy rolled toward her in bed and asked, "Where have you gone?" and Christine refused to answer: it was due to encroaching illness. After more testing, the people who loved and cared about Christine started using another word, but I don't think I ever heard her say it: dementia. There was no telling when her withdrawal and refusal became a condition. For some time, Christine as we knew her had been taking her leave.

> Had a bit of snow; but it's gone now. . . . & Mr. Squirrel seems to like the food I left out for him. . . . even chased away another one who wanted to eat & came out in the rain to nibble!!!! The other squirrel is looking for acorns!!!

It dawned on me that early symptoms of her condition were what had opened the gap between Mercy and Christine into which another person had fit.

> MC hasn't replied to any of emails. . . . . . she makes me feel Un-Wanted.

With the diagnosis, I knew that I had failed to grasp the source and extent of the change in Christine. She must have sensed she was slipping. No wonder she fixed her nails into whatever she could hold, no wonder she fixed her eyes on Mercy and couldn't look away. I imagined her following Mercy around at that school event, waiting and waiting for a feeling to come—recognition, belonging, rightness—and for the feeling never to arrive. None of it felt right. And yet she didn't tell anyone for so long. Maybe she couldn't admit it to herself. Maybe she wasn't aware. Whatever the reason, for months, maybe years, she was alone inside her own fugitive mind.

For an unknowable stretch of time before the breakup, Christine had been pulling away. Not on purpose. It wasn't always obvious. The disease acted in secret, carrying out its own awful deception.

My neurology appointment today. . . . Jamie drove b/c she
knew where it was & Abbie showed up, too!!!! They were
allowed in the room where I met Mr. doc. . . . . he was a
VERY NICE MAN who seemed to appreciate me. . . . . he
asked the 2 women what they knew about me. . . . . . Jamie
said things I had heard before. . . . . Abbie said there was a
Very Painful Breakup and I didn't seem to be moving
on. . . . . The doc said "Yankee" and smiled. . . . . he asked
me a lot of questions. . . . He said I had loss of concentration & b/c I said 1913 instead of 2013. . . . . I had to spell
the word World backwards!!!! Follow up on the 18th of
December. . . .

will mail your presents tomorrow!!!! They may not get there in time for Christmas. . . . . . but they will be liked!!!!

I have had two Manhattens (sp?). . . . . I wanted the white lights for Christmas; but they seem to have blown out!!!

I crashed on the ice in my driveway & scraped my nose. . . it bled all the way to Hannaford. . . . . my pinky finger is a bloody mess. . . . I also cut up my right hand!!!!! Put some salt water on my nose; because, the Ocean water is good for healing & it looks a little better now. . . . . but sore!!!!

5 Blankets now!!!! Because it's very cold upstairs. . . . . & wear socks all night!!!! CATCHING FIRE isn't as engaging as the first book!!!! But disruption in some Districts!!!!!

PO closed on NY-day. . . . . will try tomorrow to send you your things. . . . .

Love,

C

J amie went up to Ogunquit to assess the situation. Christine was subsisting on frozen steaks, pizza, and a lot of red wine. The cabin was littered with trash. The pipes had already frozen once.

> the living room was wet. . . . . . the nice fellow moped it up!!!! He said he would have to break down the ceiling & look to see if other water had accumulated else where.

There was no plan to prevent the pipes, or Christine herself, from freezing again. What's more, Christine was hallucinating, Jamie said. She was seeing penises on the walls. Christine's life had veered into a dire nosedive. And yet, for some reason, Mercy laughed.

"This isn't funny, Mercy," Jamie said, her voice edged with frustration.

What Jamie didn't know was that there really were penises on the walls. Back when Mercy and Christine used to visit Christine's mom in Maine, they joked about the bathroom wallpaper. Mercy sat on the toilet and called out to Christine, who half pretended not to see them: the pronounced long shapes in the repeated swirly pattern of lines that looked, to Mercy at least, like rows of dicks scribbled on the wall. Dicks! Mercy found it hilarious.

Christine wasn't hallucinating. She was double-voicing. And I realized that if voices are expansive enough to contain other people's words, they can also carry various tracks of our own. Christine intermingled two versions of herself, separated by time, abandonment, and atrophy.

Remnants of her past voice survived. They contained everything she had ever loved. Even with all the dreadful forgetting, that voice remembered and still, now and then, had the capacity to sound.

Christine no longer sent me manila envelopes filled with poems, but she was still, in a way, writing poetry. In 2014, she wrote:

> I went to Trader Joes in Kittery for XC ski boots. . . . . . they didn't have any.
>
> 55 degrees here. . . . . maybe I can go out when it 70 & smoke my water pipe!!!!
>
> Found some gray tinted old fashioned glasses on mr cat!!!!
>
> Re-potted my cactus plants. . . . . hope they get stronger!!!!
>
> Ataturk is about to get Turkey Westernized. . . . . . it's tough reading about Istanbul b/c M&I were there!!!!

I was part of a workshop once with the poet Paul Tran, who told us that form is the way a poet makes their interiority known. Nothing is an accident. I told myself that Christine was still a poet, even if her email wasn't necessarily meant to be a poem. I noticed the form of her lines, where repeated marks had taken the place of terminal punctuation. With the exception of the single dot at the end of the first sentence, she needed no fewer than four periods now to end her lines, four exclamation points to convey her feeling, and yet still, her lines wouldn't close. No punctuation was terminal; no flimsy symbol could stop her.

I noticed all the proper nouns that Christine had clustered in the first and last lines of her note. I wondered if there was something about the sturdiness of the tall letters that spoke to Christine, an effect that intertwined in her mind with the writer she loved, Arundhati Roy, who used capitalization to imbue everyday words with extra strength. Kittery is a place in Maine, but the word also smuggled in the name of Christine's cat, the Bad Kitty, whose death seemed, at the time, to undo her. Had her brain snagged on the sound and look of the word, some part of her sensing that it contained a double meaning? The image reappears with "mr cat," the honorific a secret language with Mercy. I don't know if this cat she was talking about was real or a figment of her imagination, but his glasses were tinted gray, a dingy, darkening film between him and the world. I pictured the cacti, their thick skins and outstretched arms, and Christine ministering to them, stoic plants covered in spikes. I noticed the rhythm of hope and disappointment, action and emptiness. "I went," "maybe I can go," only to realize "they didn't have any," "it's tough." And yet still, there were all those exclamation points. They held her decline and her energy to resist it. And then Christine and Mercy appear as a couple in the final moment of her poem. "M&I." Together, no space between them, connected by an intricate, looping line, a clasp. "M&I were there!!!!"

Boots, water pipe, glasses, cactus plants. I thought of Bakhtin's understanding of the relationship between language and the object it names. The dynamic is never direct. It's prismatic, a refraction that cuts through the atmosphere between the word and the object, in a "play of light and shadow." The atmosphere is filled with all the other words that have ever been spoken about the object, by every other person who has sent language in its direction. The word, in this sense, forms a "ray of light," and the atmosphere around the word is what "makes the facets of the image sparkle."

All those lines and dots in Christine's writing were seams I pried open to create room for a different meaning I wanted to imagine. The symbols made space for the two of us to coexist in the gap between the depleted parts of her life where her sentences faded mid-thought and the declarative force that remained despite—or maybe because of—her mind's change. When we talked, I pictured tiny exclamation points spilling from the phone when I heard her eerily monotone voice on the other end, especially when she paused for so long I thought she'd lost interest and just hung up. I imagined the unspoken words that hovered inside her punctuational excess. Her dots marked the entrance to a secret channel, a pathway that suctioned me in.

"I went to Trader Joes in Kittery for XC ski boots" ... *because Mercy and I used to drive into the woods together each February, in black wool caps with white iron-on letters spelling out the word "moxie" along the edge. Once we were out on the narrow paths, Mercy skied up ahead, and I watched her push forward, listened to the steady swish of her skis against the snow, her exhales, her laughter. "How we doing, Christine?" she asked.* "They didn't have any."

"Found some gray tinted old fashioned glasses on mr cat!!!!" *But now the Bad Kitty is gone, and when she died, something was lost within me, too. Maybe parts of me were already shrinking, fading, erasing themselves by then—but I didn't know it, at least not for sure. Mercy's bags of black licorice are gone from the cabinet.* "Re-potted my cactus plants . . . hope they get stronger!!!!" *I already lost the cat and Mercy, too.*

"Ataturk is about to get Turkey Westernized" . . . *Turkey. France. Paris. Berlin. Bosnia. San Francisco. Pennsylvania. Ogonquit. We were together for 17 years.* "it's tough reading about Istanbul b/c M&I were there!!!!" *M&I. M&I. M&I.*

As I watched Christine change into a person I didn't recognize, I was holding on to someone, too. Her words were a gateway to the Christine I missed and remembered from before, my own wind telephone to a different time, an earlier her.

Bakhtin used the term "loophole" to describe this property of language that allows us to reimagine a story's end. He was always looking for loopholes in novels. I notice them in everyday speech. Air quotes create loopholes, when we say something serious in a silly accent, add a winking face to our emoji strings, create dialogues with pretend interlocutors. Loopholes are words with "a sidewards glance" that turn utterances into disputed texts, alive with potential and collaboratively produced, which can be exciting but also fraught, because it suggests there is always more to the story, that no one author gets the last word.

The word with a loophole presents itself as an ultimate word, "but in fact it is only the penultimate word and places after itself only a conditional, not a final, period," wrote Bakhtin.

A loophole undermines the period's capacity to bring a sentence to a close. We can only ever get to the second-to-last word. With a loophole, "language preserves an otherwise in itself."

"Nothing conclusive has yet taken place in the world, the ultimate word of the world and about the world has not yet been spoken, the world is open and free."

We have not yet reached the end.

amie sensed that Christine wasn't telling Andy the whole story of what was going on—not even close. And she knew the time and location of Christine's therapy appointments. She felt she had no choice. She needed Andy to understand the seriousness of the situation. So, one day, she barged into his office when he was mid-session with Christine.

"I have to tell you what's going on," she told Andy. "Has she even told you that she has been diagnosed with cognitive decline? That she's been put on leave from school?"

Andy's eyes got huge. He had absolutely no idea. Christine had been spending her sessions impressing him with details about the Syrian president or the book she was reading. Meanwhile, she had a hard time tying her shoes and had been spotted on the road near campus, standing in the middle of the street, utterly oblivious to the cars whizzing by.

Winter–Spring 2014

Chaser
Jamie came to my session w/Andy & said
some hard things. . . . . like "I am in denial of
my cognitive decline." And "shit happens to
people."

Send me a photo of Lissa w/her necklace
on!!!!!
xoxoxoxo
C

> What did Andy think of what Jamie said?
> What do YOU think of what she said? I
> don't know Jamie well, but she doesn't strike
> me as someone who would say things
> intended to hurt you—she must be doing it
> because she loves you and thinks it's
> important for you to hear. Are you feeling
> symptoms of cognitive decline? Are there
> things the doctor told you you should be
> doing? Ugh, it all sounds really tough.
> Pictures coming soon!
> xoxo
> C

Chaser
I put aside THE QUEEN'S LOVER & am
reading the book about the abduction of a
nun!!!! Who wails, loudly. . . . . & beats her
head against her confinement. Curious to see
how she fares. . . . .
    It's raining here. . . . . A standoff between
the crows & the squirrel. . . . . he won!!!!
Although when they flew away, he got scared
& looked to the tree!!!
    Bought chicken teriyaki for my
supper. . . . . . Hope it doesn't give me bad
guts tomorrow. . . .
Love
C

Hey, Christiner—
I haven't heard from you all week.
Are you doing OK? Is the weather
starting to look like Spring yet?
xoxoxo
C

Chaser
I got you package today in my PO Box . . . . .
the book is amazing!!!
   M&I were lovers in the gorgeous city!!!!!
@ 124 Baker St & the Metro Hotel . . . .
where we would stay on trips . . . . . the back
garden was beautiful!!!! And we would visit
w/ you & Lissa!!!! And play the name
game. . . . . . Lissa & I always won!!!!
   What are you reading?????
Love
C

Hey Christine!
I'm writing to double check that you're
getting this email, since Chas and I haven't
heard from you in a long time! We miss you!
I'm also cc'ing Chas. Can you reply to both
of us so we can test that you're getting our
notes and that we're receiving yours?
XOX
Lissa

Christiner—
I just heard from Lissy (who heard from
Jamie) that you're having email troubles.
We haven't heard back from you.
Did you get this?
xoxoxo
Chaser

Christine could barely navigate the computer. It wasn't safe anymore for her to live alone. Jamie found a memory care facility in a converted bed-and-breakfast that had room for Christine—the Carriage House.

I knew she wouldn't have a computer up there. She'd finally have to convert to text. I sent her one last email to see how she was holding up. Her response was short and to the point.

Not holding up OK!!!
Love,
C

Fall 2014–Winter 2015
Texts between Christine and Mercy

Nov 7, 2014, at 8:51
Mercy when will me and bring me back to
ogunquit,?

Nov 8, 2014, at 14:29
Mercy i have to stay another night here
Mercy soccer Plays behind the line can we do
that /with fh?
Mercy when will rescue me and take me
back to ogunquit?

Nov 10, 2014, at 07:42
Mercy i need to stay another night hear
I love you!

Nov 16, 2014, at 16:21
Mercy I need to stay here another night!!
Mercedes thats your name! !

Nov 16, 2014, at 16:36
Hi C. How are you today?
What book are you reading?

Nov 19, 2014, at 06:56
Mercy I need to spr boom

Dec 1, 2014, at 15:20
C ~ hi. Snow there? Do you remember
Mister Biggs? I am writing comments slips
for 411 writers. Oh my. How are you?

Dec 1, 2014, at 17:00
Merrry do you xx........

Dec 2, 2014, at 08:27
Hi c!

Dec 2, 2014, at 11:31
Merrrry you wwwant tu sacab down a xo

Dec 4, 2014, at 07:45
Goodmorning C ~ Welcome to winter cold!
Did package from Brooklyn arrive to you
yet? Hi hi.

Dec 4, 2014, at 18:34
Are you watching the news about protests
because of ferguson?

Dec 5, 2014, at 17:22
Hello?

Dec 7, 2014, at 10:42
Merrrry you wwamo to winter sab down tu
yyon

Dec 10, 2014, at 14:49
Merrrrry you wwant to pa pc amm xxoo

Dec 11, 2014, at 14:27
Merrrry you watching the pictures of Laurie
and Mom
What's the .ho uhm xn

Dec 14, 2014, at 17:44
Hi C. Jamie and I are coming up tomorrow!
See you then. We leave at 3 so will get to you
by 5. Can we take you out for dinner?

Dec 20, 2014, at 12:31
Merrrrry do you wwamon to xo

Dec 20, 2014, at 15:56
Can you answer your phone? Thanks!

Dec 22 2014, at 14:01
Merrrrry wwie hrs a hopeful heart

Dec 26, 2014, at 10:33
I have snow up @ an

Dec 26, 2014
Nice !!! Beautiful ~.

Jan 1, 2015, at 01:15
And it is a new year.
Thinking of you. Xo
Mercy

Feb 11, 2015, at 15:34
Christine. ? Are you okay up there? I have
not heard from you in a while. XoMercy

From inside a dialogue, you never know when you're reading the last word.

You should come soon," Mercy had said, when she called to tell us that Christine was mostly silent now, that she only spoke a word or two here and there, and that we had to get there quickly if we wanted to see her again. She actually said those words, "if you want to see her again."

When we arrived a couple of days later and climbed out of the car in Mercy's driveway, I smelled the barbeque she was preparing for dinner. It'd been forever since Chas and I had a spontaneous night without the kids, let alone an unplanned cross-country trip, so there was something about rolling up to Mercy's place as the sun went down that made me feel strangely young, even though the reason we were here felt like we were suddenly old.

Mercy's hair was threaded with silver, wound into a little bun. She wasn't alone when we got there. The new girlfriend was with her, Lisa. Lisa was so happy to meet us. I saw them laugh together at the sink, Lisa reach into the drawer and hand Mercy a serving spoon, the two of them hovering around each other's bodies the way you do when a relationship is new. I couldn't help it. The way Lisa put her arm around Mercy's shoulder looked to me like bragging. I found myself thinking, unkindly: *she doesn't belong to you.*

Chas kept Mercy company at the grill, rotating skewers of chicken and vegetables, and Lisa was occupied with the sides. I told them I would settle into the room for a few minutes and stepped quietly down the stairs into the basement. Picking through long, flat boxes of broken oil pastels, jars of scissors and X-Acto knives, rackets and balls, I searched for Christine. Maybe a book she taught in her senior seminar on love and protest, or some seashells from the beach in Ogunquit. A stash of letters tucked high on a shelf. I poked around in a small box for her silver rings. I found nothing.

The next morning, Mercy, Chas, and I drove up to Maine. The Carriage House still had the look of the bed-and-breakfast it once was, with an old-timey sign outside, shelves stacked with hardback books, patterned cloths thoughtfully arranged on tables, and the smell of roasted chicken being prepared for lunch. I had expected something a lot more medical. The only giveaways that this was not, in fact, a country inn were all the huge recliners clustered in twos and threes and the faraway expressions on the crinkly faces of the people enfolded in them.

When Chas walked through the sun porch and into the common room, Christine looked up from where she was sitting, made a sound like a cough and the beginning of his name, and started silently to cry. A cat named Angel tiptoed across her lap. Spotting Christine there, in an overstuffed chair, I realized that I had never seen her sitting on anything so indulgent. She was a person of hard edges and sharp angles, not soft surfaces. If she were a piece of furniture, she'd be, I don't know, a bench.

We told Christine we'd brought some pictures and asked if she wanted to see. Christine bent her knees to make a surface of her thighs. She was wearing men's track pants with maroon stripes down the side, which was normal. She didn't have her glasses, which was not. Without them, she looked younger than I was used to, an unfamiliar wide-openness in her eyes. I wasn't sure how well she could see the images she started leafing through in slow motion.

She was almost done when a man approached and presented me with a picture of his own: an old woman in a silver frame. He made noises that told me she was his wife and he loved her. I told myself that she was already dead because that was so much less sad than to imagine him here clutching her picture, and her elsewhere, lunching on something other than roasted chicken with someone other than this forthcoming man.

An aide came over with a fruity popsicle that melted faster than Christine could eat it, dripping sugary water into a white cardboard bowl. A week or so before we came, Christine had been sent to the hospital for aspirating her food. When Mercy found out, she got someone to cover her class and went up to Maine right away. She thought she could bring Christine back to the Carriage House once the hospital cleared her to return, but Mercy was told that she wasn't allowed to take Christine in her car. Transport had to be arranged by the care facility. So Mercy drove to pick up chocolate ice cream instead, and she sat with Christine while she ate small spoonfuls. Swallowing was difficult, and it would only get worse.

I kissed Christine on her cheeks, shoulders, and arms, and though the absence of "I love you" was a language that carried over into her friendships, I couldn't help but tell her I did, again and again. I asked if it was okay and she said yes, but Mercy had already told me that she'd been mixing up yes and no.

"Christine, you're probably hating this," I said, speaking not of the squishy chair or even that she was here, at this place, but of the fact that I was being so corny. Running my hand up and down her arms where the muscles had softened, I could sense the bones underneath. It occurred to me that the tattoo spelling "voice" across her collarbone was just about the only voice she had left. Mercy's got a matching one near her ankle.

"You're like, 'Lissa, what's gotten into you?'" I said, and I thought about how her voice interlaced with my words, how my words made room for both of us, filled to overflowing.

I said the words I wanted to hear, quoting the New England vowels I knew I'd have been met with had I tried for such unrestrained affection before all this. I produced two sides of a half-uttered conversation that was, at once, ordinary and magical. For so long now, Christine had been speaking in a voice I didn't recognize in letters I sometimes had to force myself to skim. I longed to hear the words she once possessed and realized that now, to do that, I would have to be the one to speak them.

"I hope it's okay."

"Yes."

Yes, no, yes, no.

I couldn't be sure she meant it.

On that visit to the Carriage House, it didn't take long to realize that the people who ran the place wanted permission for Christine to get a feeding tube. It could prevent another dangerous incident of Christine aspirating food into her lungs, and besides, staff at the Carriage House believed that dementia patients even as far along as she was could still enjoy a good quality of life. They told Jamie that Christine had visited another resident who'd been hospitalized, to sit with him and keep him company. "She's still here," they said. Chas was upset. Before the dementia had become this advanced, Christine had signed a paper declining forced nutrition. She could no longer string together a sentence, follow a thought, or make it to the bathroom. As far as Chas was concerned, she had made her wishes clear.

I wasn't so sure. Didn't she light up when her cat, Angel, crept across her lap? Didn't that beam of sun feel nice when it shone on her, in the soft chair, through the pretty window? A doctor told Jamie that a feeding tube would make Christine more comfortable. Jamie also told us that just a few weeks prior, when Christine had still been able to speak in short sentences, Jamie had asked her, "Are you hungry?" and Christine answered, "I'm starving." Weren't those still her words, too?

In *Brilliant Imperfection*, Eli Clare writes that people who live with disabilities that grow more significant over time draw lines in the sand beyond which they determine that life would be intolerable, but then their conditions change, and their lines can shift, too. Clare cites another writer, Nancy Mairs, who has multiple sclerosis. At various times, Mairs believed that she could not possibly live without walking on the beach, teaching, driving, being able to put on and remove her own underwear, and yet, one by one, Mairs adapted to these changes: "I go on being, now more than ever, the woman I once thought I could never bear to be."

Christine's caregivers kept urging us to record our conversations, as if the videos would be a kind of proof that would convince us to do whatever we could to extend her life. "Quick, take a video!" they insisted. "Then you'll be able to look at it and see how great she's doing!"

And so I have a video now in a text thread on my phone, with Christine flipping through the pictures we'd brought, looking at the four of us at Chas's and my wedding, in Big Sur, on a trip to New York City. And then you hear me, in Christine's voice: "Can you stop chatting, so I can concentrate?" On the cusp of losing her, I imagined words to hold her here with us just a little bit longer, turning her sentences over in my mouth to express who she was, who we had been. We would need to carry her voice from here.

For me, the sadness that came with her retreat was expected. What I hadn't expected was the feeling of redolence. Our words, filling the silent space. Christine, reminiscent of herself.

I have heard stories of dying people surging into sudden lucidity at the very end, almost as if the fullest, clearest version of themselves sneaks back into the room for one last appearance. This didn't exactly happen with Christine. She didn't move from her chair. Her eyes didn't clear. She barely said a word. But sitting with her, I felt an enormous vitality. And I understood at least part of its source. I imagined a flood of voices rushing into her soul, every word she'd spoken or heard or read or written or felt or inherited, among them the ones the four of us had shared. A final gathering before her leave.

At some point in my pursuit of Bakhtin, I emailed Caryl Emerson, the translator and scholar. I wanted to talk to someone who knew his work deeply and had done everything she could to inhabit his voice. She replied within minutes and said she would be happy to talk but not for a few days, because her own father had just died. When we spoke the next week, she told me some of her father's last words: "I'm looking for the location of my awareness. I think that love is there all the same." Of course, she said, Bakhtin was with her in her father's final moments. "Bakhtin really believed if you could get hold of a word, it had enormous reanimating power," she told me. Bakhtin helps us talk to the living and talk to the dead. The theorist of language had become, for me at least, and maybe Caryl, too, a philosopher of love.

Caryl told me she was finishing up an afterword to a brand-new collection of Bakhtin's writing and offered to send me an advance copy. The publication would be called *The Dark and Radiant Bakhtin*. It was a compilation of wartime notebooks he'd kept in the 1940s, with commentary from scholars from around the world.

When I opened the draft Caryl sent me, I saw that in his note-books, Bakhtin—like Christine—wrote elliptically, in fragments. The essays contained in the volume weren't intended to be pub-lished in this form. They were Bakhtin's musings, partly formed ideas he was still figuring out in longhand. "In the broken rhythm of the fragments," wrote Irina Sandomirskaia about his feverish notes, "one hears a soliloquy all the time interrupting itself, as if somebody else, some other person, were speaking to the author from the inside of his own writing."

It was in one of those notebooks that Bakhtin started to work out the difference between what he called Great Experience and Small Experience. Great Experience takes place outside the ordi-nary time and space of life, in moments "of eccentricity, at infer-nal, heavenly . . . and purgatorial points." Great Experience strives to see in everything a kind of "unfinalizedness and freedom," wrote Bakhtin. "Everything is alive, everything speaks."

Small Experience isn't like that at all. In Small Experience, there is only one speaker, who treats every other person as if they are "closed . . . answerless and silent," a mere object of thought to be devoured, subjugated, consumed. In Small Experience, the other person has already spoken their last word. No "inner open kernel is left . . . no inner infinity."

Sitting with Chas, Mercy, and Christine in that sunny back room at the Carriage House felt like one of those eccentric points Bakhtin talked about, spectral and golden. I listened for Christine's inner infinity, so we could keep walking further and further alongside each other in life. She said almost nothing, and we hung on her every remembered word, suspended in a place that was at once Great and Small, sad and a reprieve from sadness. And I wanted to imagine that Christine was feeling a kind of infinity, too, that we four were producing it together. Because we were there. Including, finally, the one of us who mattered most.

"Brown Eyes," Christine said, two of the five words she spoke over the course of the hours we spent with her that day. Yes. No. Angel. Brown. Eyes.

"Brown Eyes" was for Mercy. Flatly stated, connected to nothing and everything.

"Yes," said Mercy, whose eyes are dark and warm.

"Brown Eyes" was the thing spoken out loud, "I love you" the subtext.

We sounded like ourselves again. Her voice filled the room emptied by her retreat, reincarnating this foursome that held us, before and now.

I shouldn't have been surprised by the mix of sweetness and pain,

failings in others, and in ourselves.

Christine had warned me on my wedding day.

There will be times of wounding and the necessity for
healing.
In conversation there will be the unspoken.

There is also the reverse. In the unspoken, there is conversation.
In this silence, her voice rolled from our tongues.

Long before Bakhtin's ideas were translated and sent around the world, almost all the others who pulled up their chairs in his living room had died. There were Voloshinov and Medvedev, of course. And Matvei Kagan, a founding member of the Circle, who died at forty-eight of a heart attack, which his family insists was triggered by terror that his own arrest was imminent. Boris Mikhailovich Zubakin was arrested for attending Kagan's funeral in Moscow, which violated the terms of his exile. Within a year, Zubakin was dead, too, in a prison camp where he'd been sent for counterrevolutionary activity.

Only the pianist Maria Veniaminovna Yudina survived to old age. Her playing was said to sound like a sermon. Yudina recited poems by dissident writers during her concert intermissions. Through words and music, she double-voiced her critique of the Soviet regime. There's a story that says that one day, Joseph Stalin heard her play live on the radio and demanded a recording of the concerto for himself. Yudina was whisked from her bed in the middle of the night and driven to a studio where a small ensemble awaited. They recorded the piece right then and there, so Stalin's men could deliver the copy to him by morning. He'd never know that the version he possessed was not the original performance but a repetition, a citation of itself.

And then there was Bakhtin's wife, Elena. She died four years before him, and finally, he moved to a flat in Moscow, where they had wanted to be for so long, at the center of things. It is said that he took up residence at 21 Krasnoarmeyskaya Street, and that the address made him happy, because Elena's grave plot had the same number, 21. Apparently numbers were special to them, too. In that apartment he reclined, on a couch in his robe, "receiving the callers."

In an interview just two years before he died, Bakhtin reflected on the arc of his life: "There has to be many-voicedness," he said. "There has to be, and there was." The interviewer pressed him on the matter of authorship with respect to the disputed texts. He dodged the question. "I really did not know that everything would turn out the way it has. And then, what significance does all this have—authorship, a name? Everything that has been created in this half-century, on this barren ground, under this unfree sky, all of it is, to a greater or lesser degree, flawed." Everything we create, and every creator.

It is said that Bakhtin's final words were "I go to thee." There's been much debate about who he was talking to, in what may have been his last utterance of all: God? Elena? I like to think he wasn't addressing any one person or divinity. I like to imagine that in his final release from life, he rushed toward all the people whose voices had shaped his, the ones who came before him, the ones who lived alongside him, and the ones, like me, who found him after he was already gone.

With illness and death around us, Chas and I started going to services at a synagogue in the Mission, not far from the Rite Spot where we had met up with Mercy and Christine for the first time. Over time, we became close friends with the rabbis, a couple around our age. When Michael was young and trying to figure out whether he was suited for a religious path, he asked an elder he knew from the community how to decide. The rabbi said: "Get close to death."

One morning at a Saturday service, I ran into Michael and he looked tired. I asked how he was doing. He told me that one of his congregants had just died from cancer.

She had two sons, eighteen months apart. The family had decided to do the b'nei mitzvah early, so she could be there. When the day arrived, the mom was too sick to leave the hospital bed they'd set up for her at the house. They held the service in the next room.

Before the ceremony started, before the chanting, the bending of knees and bowing of heads and murmuring of prayers, before the singing and cries of "Mazel tov!," Michael took the two boys and their dad quietly into their mother's room. They nestled the Torah up against her body in the bed for a few moments.

Forty of their loved ones gathered to witness the two boys, reading aloud the same lines that people had been reciting on that same day of the Hebrew calendar for thousands of years. If one of the boys mispronounced a word, Michael gently repeated it correctly, as is the tradition, so the story was perfect.

To avoid losing his place, each boy ran a special silver pointer called a *yad* along the lines of text as he chanted the words right to left. When reading from the Torah, Jews use a *yad* instead of a fingertip because a fingertip is coated with oils that, over years and decades and centuries, mar the letters that a calligrapher painstakingly inked onto the scrolls. While all words are already lived in, this is especially true for ancient ones. Even if the point of rereading the same stories each year is to see how their meanings change every time, there still needs to be some way to make sure the actual letters on the parchment don't blur or disappear from use.

"How are the boys doing?" I asked stupidly after Michael told me this story. Their mom had just died days before. How did I think they were doing?

"There is an earthquake right now that is shaking this family," Michael told me. "It is so brutal and cruel. And it is causing a tsunami to form on the other side of the ocean. Waves are building and building from a place far away, and the waves will come, and they will hit, in different ways, on different shores. As they should. It's unpredictable. It's gonna hit them. Those waves will come and knock them down. They will have to get up, and walk through."

They will have to talk through, too. Maybe repeating lines in an ancient language they barely understand will help. Maybe it won't.

They will have to find ways to stay in dialogue with a loved one who is no longer there to speak words of her own. Her words, and theirs, will have to find one another, connected to nowhere and everywhere, carried on the wind.

One night, Emily went out to a café with a friend. They were talking and catching up. The friend asked how the kids were doing, and then: "I want to ask you, how's Jonnie?"

"I can't believe you just said that," Emily said. She put down her coffee cup. "Thank you so much."

"Well," the friend said, "you would know."

She'd opened a loophole. The trick was in the tense: a word with a sidewards glance into the past and future that unlocked an everlasting present for Emily and Jonnie together.

The wind telephone is a loophole, and when I first heard about it, I wondered: For the loved ones who keep going back, is the lost voice frozen in time? Does a child return to the booth one day and find a parent who is younger than they are now, like when the poet Natasha Trethewey dreams of her mother who died decades before, "always I am older than she is, older than she ever was"? Can a lover pick up the phone and experience the voice of a spouse who is the age of their child?

The question Emily's friend asked held an answer. The voices on the other end of the wind telephone contain within them all of time, because we draw our voices not from inside our isolated selves but from the great flow of words that washes over us from the world. A flow each of us adds to, with every word we say.

A medium once told Emily that dimes are a message from Jonnie. Whenever she finds one—in the box of winter boots in the entryway to the house, behind the cushion of a couch, glinting among blades of grass on the lawn—she takes it as a sign that he's okay, or she is, or that he's with them. Sometimes I find one, too, and I'll slide it into my back pocket as if he's telling me, "Yes, keep going," because I so hope that's what he would say if he were here. Andrew, the guy Emily started dating a few years after Jonnie died, even he'll find a dime now and then. The first time he came for dinner with the kids, Andrew asked Emily which was Jonnie's chair. "I don't want to sit in his place," Andrew said, and he has extended that graceful intention into his relationships with the kids ever since, when he built a shelf for Sadie's toys, went to the kids' lacrosse games, nodded off on the bean bag while they watched a movie so Emily could go out for dinner with a friend. Watching Andrew with the kids, I have often thought how much Jonnie would have liked him, and so I was not surprised to learn that sometimes, he and Emily will find a dime when they're together. It makes them wonder.

There's a hill up the street from my house that's burnt brown most of the year and golf-course green for the few weeks it gets around to raining in San Francisco. It's where Jonnie's sister, Jeanne, held a ceremony after he died. It's where I go to visit Jonnie because sometimes I feel him there, a brimming, an invitation. Lately, when I am lucky enough to sense him opening the sky like that, I think of a line from Ingrid Rojas Contreras: "There is nothing to do but wait for the wave of devotion to pass."

A wave like that has the power to overwhelm the rules by which time normally operates. The journalist Marjorie Williams, dying of liver cancer, wrote about her last Halloween for a column in the

Washington Post. She'd loaded up on pain meds so she could help her nine-year-old child, Alice, get ready. She covered Alice with body glitter, slicked on lip gloss, and watched her daughter head out with friends.

> Alice looked back and tossed me a radiant smile. She had become my glimmering girl: She looked like a rock star. She looked like a teenager. . . . She thundered down the stairs in those shoes, and as the front door slammed behind her, it came to me—what fantasy I had finally, easily entered this Halloween. I'd just seen Alice leave for her prom, or her first real date. I'd cheated time, flipping the calendar five or six years into the future. The character I'd played was the 52-year-old mother I will probably never be.

A loophole. It allows Williams to glimpse a feeling just on the other side of the barrier of loss, and in my mind's eye, I replace her single period with Christine's "!!!!"

"One of the things that makes these calls so poignant to me," said the radio producer Miki Meek about the recordings she heard in Itaru's booth, "is all the understated ways that people are actually saying, 'I love you.'" In the loophole of what is not spoken out loud, the absence of "I love you," like Mercy said, is a language of its own.

Filling speech with other people's words can be an act of love. But it is also an act of power that both gives and takes away, a "blow" and a "gift," Bakhtin wrote. And we will never be sure if we did right by Christine, when Jamie gave the go-ahead for the feeding tube. It didn't really matter in the end. The minds of people with dementia aren't the only organs that forget how to function. So can their throats and lungs. After the procedure to insert Christine's feeding tube, she died the next day.

There was a memorial service at the school where Mercy and Christine taught, in September, three months after she died. The timing felt significant. Fall was Christine's favorite season, the towering trees around campus aflame with color, new books to assign, essays to annotate, games to play. For decades, Christine had been a beloved teacher and coach. Over time, she'd receded from campus life, but colleagues and students had gone to see her at the Carriage House—Donna from IT, who'd set her up with email; a beloved graduate who flew in from Israel. The school dedicated its 2015 Martin Luther King program to Christine, and the week she died, the flag on campus flew at half-mast.

When Chas and I arrived for the service, Mercy asked me to go with her to her classroom to print out her speech. I kept wanting her to turn away from the screen and face me, to start remembering. I wanted her to tell me about our vacation in Big Sur. The time we got into a fight over Zidane's headbutt in the 2006 World Cup. Or when we used to play the Name Game, where you put famous people's names in a hat and then try to get each other to guess. One ridiculous time we decided to fill the hat with concepts instead, and then we died laughing over the pretentious absurdity of trying to act out words like "envy" and "disarmament." But Mercy didn't seem to want to remember. She fixed typos in her speech and fielded phone calls from her parents and sister who'd be arriving soon from Pennsylvania.

And while I realized that it was the underlying dementia that likely broke up her relationship with Christine, for Mercy, the diagnosis couldn't turn back time. Christine had retreated so inexplicably and then unleashed such relentless jealousy and bitterness. Her desperate sexual disinhibition made Mercy's skin crawl. Her inability to let their relationship go metastasized into a kind of harassment. All of this had gone on for years. Mercy now understood that when Christine had stalked her after their relationship had ended, it was at least in part the dementia that made her hang on so relentlessly to a life and version of herself she couldn't bear to lose. But that knowledge couldn't repair the damage. At the end of Christine's life, Mercy went to see her, talked to the doctors on her behalf, rolled Christine in a wheelchair to visit the ocean. But Mercy couldn't fully return to her or let her back in.

"I asked you if you missed anything about us," Christine had written to Mercy after the breakup. "You say it may take time to miss it."

Mercy wasn't ready for missing at this memorial where not as many people as I wanted had come, where Lisa sat in the front row.

A student sang "Across the Great Divide." Christine's high school boyfriend gave a speech about their childhood, as did her brother, David. Chas and I spoke, too, and Jamie, and other colleagues and friends. And then, partway through the program, Mercy stepped up to the lectern and unfolded her paper.

> There were inkwells of deep green, of cobalt blue, of golden gate orange. Occasionally there was a pencil ~ thin tipped & mechanical as the years went along. After a trip

to Japantown in San Francisco, there were fine pens, sleek and modern.

Mercy is an English teacher. She knew what she was doing when she chose to form her sentences this way—"there was" this, "there was" that—avoiding "she" and "I" entirely. She quoted former students, colleagues, Christine herself. It took three pages of the memorial speech before Mercy mentioned herself at all, and it struck me that a eulogy made mostly of other people's words says a lot about how language carries memory and pain, and how we use language to avoid them. It must have taken special effort, it seemed to me from my seat in that chapel, for Mercy to write so many of her own words out of the story.

When she finally did put herself into her speech at the service, it was in reference to the two boxes that Christine had left for her.

> Within the knowledge that she was dying, she placed poems, meditations, artifacts, stickers, buttons, a photo of her playing rugby once in the years before I knew her, bus tickets, her birth certificate, and a note that said something in the spirit of "You may wonder why I have saved all of this and am passing it along to you."

I remembered the last time the four of us had been together at Chas's parents' house. What a difference it might have made, had Mercy known that Christine was sick, for Mercy to be the one to set Christine up at the Carriage House and visit not sporadically but every day. That's how it could have gone, Mercy sitting with Christine on the sofa and handing her presents: a tiny spoon from when they taught in Bosnia, a shell from the beach. Mercy wouldn't expect Christine to say anything out loud. She would trust that somewhere between them, memory remained.

I knew I was only imagining the good parts of what it might have been like for Mercy to see Christine through the end of her life. But it was a memorial. This was not a place for the whole truth.

Up at the podium, Mercy was now telling us about the various people Christine would write to. She said Christine "wrote sometimes to people she knew might not write back."

I looked at Chas and thought about the times we had ignored her notes.

I looked at Mercy and thought about the letter in the dungeon of a sealed envelope on her dashboard strewn with orange peels, about all that had happened for Mercy to turn from the person who wrote with Christine by the fireplace each night into someone who stopped writing back.

Before all this, not long after the breakup, her writing still close to what it had always been, Christine sent me a poem she called "Catastrophe," to explain why she wouldn't come visit. In it, she imagined an earthquake that toppled the Golden Gate Bridge and turned

> the apartment on Baker Street and Cafe Flor
> into rubble that will be hauled away & dumped . . .
> flooded Baker Beach
> where we leapt into the Pacific
> with rusted cans and busted bottles and dirty sand
> I can hear the rumble of it
> the crash of metal and wood and waves
> 3000 miles away. The seismic shift of everything
> I had believed in. And
> I don't want to return to see the ruins.

I sensed in these lines that Christine was reaching for language to hold the enormity of her loss, the dread of a warning, the violence of a crash, the rust and bustedness of what had become of her world. And she was right, I think, to write into the ruin. She might not have been able to bring herself to come see us in San Francisco, but she faced her pain, returned to it again and again, through words. It was something she felt she had to do, and that language had the capacity to do. Bakhtin believed in this capacity of language, too, in "the fear of the immeasurable, the infinitely powerful . . . The starry sky, the gigantic material masses of the mountains, the sea, the cosmic upheavals, the elemental catastrophes—these constitute the terror that pervades ancient mythologies, philosophies, the systems of images, and language itself."

Language, pervaded by terror, loss, and love. Maybe using it to produce gigantic images—an epic flood, the Pacific Ocean, thousands of miles, a seismic shift—made it possible for Christine to survive the infinite tiny cuts of grief as life went on among the ruins.

In *Lives Other Than My Own*, Emmanuel Carrère lets himself imagine the future two lovers will never have, after one dies in a tsunami while they're vacationing in Sri Lanka.

> I imagined the two of them getting on in years, living in a lovingly tended house in an English town, taking part in its social life, going on a yearly trip to some distant country, putting together their photo albums. All that shattered. The survivor's return, the empty house. Each woman's mug with her name on it, one of them forever forlorn.

I pictured Christine alone at her kitchen table. I pictured the phone booth in Itaru's garden, the grievers standing in line, waiting for their turns, nodding in forlorn acknowledgment as one stepped out of the booth and the next stepped in.

In one of Christine's darkest moments, she had written a letter to Mercy in which she imagined some point in the future, when her brother, David, would be disposing of her ashes. She despaired that Mercy wouldn't even be there to "lean over the bridge and let what's left of me slip through your fingers to the sea." She despaired that she would be forgotten. In that same letter, Christine wrote:

> I know, from literature and history and being alive, that people have more than one lover . . . and perhaps, for some of them, love is powerful and true each time. But I am not like that. . . .
>
> And while I feel too young to never have another love in my life, I am not convinced she will write like you can, move me in ways that you have, take me into the present life like you have, lift me out of silence into voice as you have. Yes, I am now angry and hurt beyond language. But something tells me this was THE LOVE of my life.
>
> I wonder, sometimes, if my ghost will come to you, even before I am 80 or ashes and you will sense a shadow in whatever view there is on the other side of a window.

It was Mercy who drove to the crematorium to pick up Christine's ashes. A man there handed her a tiny green suede bag with the rings Christine had been wearing, and Mercy tried them on again, as she had so many times when they were together. She asked the man to divide Christine's ashes into two containers. She arranged to meet up with Christine's brother, David, and her nephew, Daniel, so they could sprinkle half her dust into the Atlantic, as Christine had wanted, and then they jumped into the water themselves, and they swam and rode the waves and told stories. Years later, Mercy remembered what their time together had felt like, "longing to have the moment pass & longing to stall the moment still."

To fulfill Christine's wish for the other half of her remains to go into the Pacific, Mercy and Lisa came to San Francisco and drove Chas and me to Baker Beach. The ashes were in the kind of small plastic box you might find on the shelf at the Container Store. Two other old friends of Christine's met us on the beach. We'd all prepared brief remarks we shared in a circle.

I based mine on a paragraph I'd found in one of Christine's letters, in which she described a sunny morning when she stopped by Mercy's place and they passed a cigarette back and forth on the porch. This was after the betrayal, the breakup, the misery, fury, and silence that followed, but before the decline had become undeniable and given a name. The rare moment of sweetness between them made it possible for Christine to believe that someday, she and Mercy could form a friendship—"a space we could live in, not with the passion of lovers, but with some kind of grace that teaches us how to heal." I read that passage out loud on the windy beach, feeling sad that Christine didn't live long enough to experience that healing but grateful at least that we were together. "We are all here," I said out loud, looking at Mercy and thinking the words "brown eyes."

In a magazine called the *Nib*, the cartoonist John Martz illustrates what he wants done to his body after death. He describes a service he read about somewhere that would turn the carbon from a cremated body into a pencil set.

> I like the idea of my friends and loved ones being given a pencil to remember me by, each one filled with potential drawings, stories, or grocery lists. Perhaps I'd be forgotten in the back of a drawer or chewed on by a forgetful relative working on a particularly tricky crossword puzzle. I'd be sharpened and worn down, eventually diminishing into a little nub, having outlived my usefulness all over again.

The comic reminds me of Bakhtin's belief that words always contain "capacity for further creative life." It reminds me of the moment at Baker Beach when police cars started circling the area and shining their lights onto the sand. We worried that they might soon come down to the shore and catch us putting human remains into the ocean, which we'd heard was against the law. So we stopped our talking, rolled up our jeans, stepped toward the water, formed Christine's powdery ashes into the shape of her initial, and watched the waves wash her letter away.

Three years after Christine died, six years after Jonnie died, Emily and I both had thirteen-year-olds and found ourselves together preparing for our children's b'nei mitzvot. This was surprising, since Chas and Jonnie weren't Jewish and Emily's German Jewish family had abandoned religious tradition a generation ago. Simone's was set for just a month before Max's, so Emily and I supported each other a lot through the process. There were aspects of going through it together that were hard. At one point I told her about our rabbis' ritual, before the service starts, to take the immediate family—the kid, siblings, parents, and grandparents—into a quiet room. Everyone stands in a circle and says a prayer as a rabbi drapes the kid with a sacred shawl called a *tallis* for the first time. Having gone through that process with Roma, forming a circle of kinship spanning three generations, I strongly recommended Emily do the same.

"Yeah, but for us that would leave just Maxine, Sadie, and me," she pointed out, and I was reminded once again of how easily we can lapse into a certain kind of obliviousness to the difference between our own lives and those of others, even the ones we know and love the most. But Emily didn't seem upset, so we let it go and she shared a draft of her parent's blessing. This was the point in the service when she would address Max in front of their whole community. The idea was to say something meaningful about who your kid is, the life you hope they'll have, and the kind of person they'll become.

> When we were in California for your fourth-grade year, you decided you wanted to go out for the Oakland co-ed kids football team. We arrived at the football stadium on a gray and rainy Sunday. You stopped for a moment under my umbrella looking out at the field below. From the top of the bleachers it was a sea of boys throwing balls around. Before continuing down towards the field you asked, "Mom, where are the girls?" I paused, wondering what to say.

Emily wasn't sure about this moment in the blessing. She didn't know if she should say what actually was going through her mind at the time: "Jonnie, are you seeing this? Do you know what's happening?" These were the types of decisions Emily was making a lot around the b'nei mitzvah: when to bring in Jonnie's voice, when to leave it unuttered. As we talked through her choices, I was struck by how much had changed, since those first terrible months and years after he died. It's not that it wasn't still sad; of course it was. But there was also a matter-of-factness to it, a bittersweetness. We wanted Jonnie there to see his magnificent Max go through this rite of passage, but I sensed that Emily knew how to make sure he would be.

Among the countless other tasks Emily had to take care of in planning for Max's day—arranging bouquets, finding a last-minute DJ, realizing she had the wrong adapter for the projector running the slideshow—there was also the matter of the candle-lighting ceremony. This is the point in a service for honoring the dead, and for Max that meant their dad and all the grandparents. For each candle, the immediate family of the remembered loved one is called up from their seats in the congregation to gather around Max and light a flame. At the ceremony, Jonnie's siblings were up there for their mom's candle and started to exit the stage until the service leader called out their father's name, and Jonnie's sister, Jeanne, who shared her brother's gallows humor, said, "Oh wait, we're in this one, too."

For Emily's part, she had to decide how to refer to herself when they lit Jonnie's candle. As each person's name was read, the service leader would state their relationship to Jonnie: his sister, his brother, his nephew, his niece. But what did Emily want to be called? If she chose widow, she told me, then everyone else would be named in relationship to Jonnie's love, and only she would be called in relation to his death. In the end, she went with wife, which Andrew agreed was the right move. "Emily, you're my girlfriend," he said, "but you're Jonnie's wife."

A few weeks prior to the event, Max sent me a draft of the speech, called a *drash*, that they were working on and asked for my feedback. They wrote that while some Jews turn to God to change the world and guide their actions, Max puts that trust in people.

> I think of God as not one person, but many people who have died and are now part of the molecules living in nature. When I take a hike on a beautiful day, with the leaves blowing around me and the cool air on my face, I can almost feel the people in my life who have died, watching over me.

Reading along, I wondered if Max would talk directly about Jonnie. I flashed back to those first days after the accident, at Sara's house in Oakland, where the family was staying when they flew from Montana to the Bay Area. The adults who gathered at the house kept having horrible, hushed conversations until Max or Sadie came into the room, and then we'd say, "Hey, wanna read a book?" or "Should we go to the park?" or "Time to take a bath," in the most normal voices we could find.

My answer about whether Max would mention their dad came in the next paragraph.

> My father died when I was almost seven. I have been with-
> out him for six years now, and I still think about what my
> and my family's life would have been like with him in it,
> every day.

I wondered how to read that line, if Max was saying that they still thought about what everyday life would have been like with their dad, or that they still thought about him every day. The space that forms between words, people, and events creates mystery, and I noticed how, in the face of that mystery, I have a tendency to slip into binary options—did Max mean *this* or *that*. I tried sensing the simultaneity instead, the experience of a childhood like Max's, shaped by the mode of speech they used in their drash, a register of "would have been," where the actual past and an alternate future hover palpably within the present.

> I imagine being able to laugh with him, and cry with him.
> I imagine being able to rant to him about the horrible day
> I was having and how I wanted it to be better. He would
> say how things will be better tomorrow and it is just one
> day. I could talk to him about how similar my laugh is to
> his, and how different it is from everyone else's but I like it
> that way. These are the things that I will never get to talk
> to my father about, no matter how hard I try.

I thought of what Rabbi Michael had said about the boys whose b'nei mitzvah he performed with their mom in the next room, in the final days of her life. He'd said that a tsunami was forming on the other side of the ocean. Waves were building from a place far away. Over time, they would crash and crash onto the family's shore. And the kids, "they will have to get up, and walk through."

"I know that my mom, sister and I have been on this journey together," Max wrote. "We have all gotten stronger and braver."

Later that evening, Michael's words returned to me as I watched Max bouncing up and down on the dance floor in their beautiful navy suit, jostled by the raucous, joyous crowd of friends, Sadie, Andrew's son, cousins, aunts, and uncles moving in unison to a song the kids knew all the words to, and there was Emily nearby, laughing easily, barefoot, moving with the music.

"There you go. Yeah, shake it, mama, shake it, mama. Ha!"

Over the years since Jonnie died, when Emily checked in with mediums now and then, she was always curious who would show up.

"It's not like I felt him right next to me in a tangible way," she said about the times when Jonnie made an appearance. "It was more like the fact of what he was saying through her was definitely him."

All sorts of uncanny things have happened on these visits, where the medium's words sounded enough like Jonnie's to provide Emily with something to hang on to, if not lasting solace. Like when a medium said Jonnie was asking where his bike had gone, and Emily had just sold it. Or when Emily was trying to decide if she should get braces for Max, "and he literally said through the medium, 'One tooth is longer than the other'"—the exact words a dentist had spoken to her just a couple of days prior. Emily swears she hadn't brought up any of these details in advance.

"What??? What???" was all I could say when she told me this story. An instinct rose up in me, to make calculations. Maybe Emily had posted something online about selling the bike. Maybe the medium googled clients before they came in to find tidbits she could use. I wasn't sure how to explain the thing about Max's braces. Maybe, knowing the kid's age, the medium took an educated guess. But then, finally, I stopped myself. Why was I trying to take a Great Experience and reduce it to something Small? I considered the other option, the other realm for experiences like this, what Bakhtin called "the realm of maximal freedom," the realm where "everything speaks" and words renew life.

Jonnie's younger brother, Pete, the one whose voice sounds exactly like his, knew about Emily's visits to the medium. He'd even come along once for a joint session. Over the years, Emily told him the things Jonnie said in her sessions, and Pete nodded, knowing the visits brought her comfort. One time, Pete and I were drinking tea in Emily's kitchen while she was out dropping off the kids, and I asked if he believed that it was Jonnie in the room with Emily and the medium, crossing over into our world for a visit. "That's not my Jonnie," Pete said. "That's hers."

I came home from Max's b'nei mitzvah to find messages from Mercy.

Ah Liss ~

I am not sure why there is so much grief unveiling itself now. I know only that today, sitting in my classroom with my seniors in the Didion elective and talking about The Year of Magical Thinking, I kept having these strange, surreal, and yet entirely crucial physical waves of feeling again, all over again, what I sometimes felt while I was leaving C, when I was visiting her in her Carriage House, when I saw her last. Lately, I have been having constant spells of remembering the last time I saw her, of feeling that there was more I could have done, that maybe if I had spoken with the Dr differently he could have allowed her to live.

And every day, I have flashes of how terribly I handled the ending of my life with C and yet perhaps I did okay with the ending of her life: how I gave her a stone to hold in her hand; how I asked her if the hospital lights were too bright; how I turned them down; how I spoke to the Dr about what she wanted; how Jamie and I stood by her bedside and waited until she slept; how I kept wondering if I should stay.

I have no fucking idea why this is all hitting me now.

And yet . . . perhaps it is a gift. This feeling. This knowing. This moment. This collage of memories. This writing to you

. . .

I am thinking about how grief comes first in the body ~ how I denied it with pleasures or numbing to survive the pain. And I wonder often now what distractions from the grief of her changing I created & chose & fell into so that I didn't have to face it all ~ the mystery of what I now see more clearly ~

I love remembering her before language left and the loop began. I love remembering the clarity of her mind to frame an argument or debate.

I have so much of her writing in boxes and folders and on notes in books I sometimes open randomly. The fire she created ~ what love was she trying to burn? And I wonder if that act was one dictated by dementia ~ the fire a violence against language. Against healing.

And I wonder ~ it is so strange what comes to mind now ~ if she had not lit that match and held that fire, if she had saved the letters ~ what would have happened differently in her mind?

The time for missing had come.

I'd finished a draft of this book. Mercy came to visit and I shared it with her. It was such a pretty day that we decided to sit out on the deck, where we could see the same backyard gardens and lines of houses that had curved around us at the wedding.

"The ocean shows up in so many places," Mercy said, looking up from the printed pages.

"Huh, you're right," I said. I hadn't noticed until she pointed it out.

"Have you read Elizabeth Bishop's 'At the Fishhouses'? It was one of Christine's favorite poems," she said. She typed the title into her phone so we could read it together.

"Maybe you can use it somewhere in the story." I began to read:

> I have seen it over and over, the same sea, the same,
> slightly, indifferently swinging above the stones,
> icily free above the stones,
> above the stones and then the world.

I forced myself to slow way down and reread the lines, to let their images take shape. Sea, stones, freedom, the world. I remembered that Christine, in her testing, had been asked to spell the word "world" backward. I noticed the echo of Jonnie's sister's lament right after he died, that "the lake and the shore were all the same for having taken his life," the cold waves indifferent to her suffering. I saw how, over time, the sea called to Christine. She came to it, over and over, scanning the coastline for a version of her life that was slipping away, willing the salty air to take her back, looking for Mercy most of all.

Something about that image jogged a memory. I went inside and got the stack of Christine's letters and emails I kept in the bottom drawer of my desk and flipped through them until I found the one I was looking for. It was an email where she wrote about the "Ocean, 54 degrees . . . ICY cold!!!"

Rereading her words, I imagined Christine charging into the water at Baker Beach with Mercy: "Went to the Main Beach to get my hand wet & licked off the salt," she wrote, and Bishop finished the thought:

> If you should dip your hand in,
> your wrist would ache immediately,
> your bones would begin to ache and your hand would burn
> as if the water were a transmutation of fire
> that feeds on stones and burns with a dark gray flame.

I thought of the fire Christine had set to incinerate the words Mercy had written for her over all of those years. I ached for who Christine had been, as a writer, friend, teacher, lover, who, from the absence of that word, formed a language of our own. And so I sifted through the words she'd left behind to find their abiding poetry. When I found a line or image that echoed or interlaced with Bishop's, it felt like discovering a fossil, proof that Christine's old self had existed—the keen reader, the poet she had been. I pictured her experiencing the bracing cold of the water, cupping her hands "to get my face wet & licking my lips." It was another of Christine's images that spilled into Bishop's . . .

> If you tasted it, it would first taste bitter,
> then briny, then surely burn your tongue.
> It is like what we imagine knowledge to be:
> dark, salt, clear, moving, utterly free,
> drawn from the cold hard mouth
> of the world . . .

I know now that our friendship would take us to dark places and yet was overwhelmingly both moving and free. It found its "verbal shape" through words: handwritten, typed, scribbled along the edges of books, stashed in the backs of closets and drawers, erased.

What helped me feel close to Christine after she was gone was the presence of a stranger, a poet she adored, contained within her speech. I'd found a loophole in our dialogue that was also a space for me to write into, to write her back into the parts of our lives she loved the most.

At some point, we have to let go of the versions of people we love who aren't with us anymore. And yet we keep talking to them, hearing them, experiencing their poetry.

"And there is no such thing as happy poetry," Bakhtin said, "and there should not be. If there is no element of death in it, if there is no element of the end, or some presentiment of death, then it is not poetry, it is a stupid rapture."

Christine's poetry opened a line into Great Experience. Books can do the same thing. My copy of Bakhtin's *Dialogic Imagination* has three sets of annotations: the ones Mercy left before she gave me the book, the ones I added for my dissertation, and then the ones I wrote when Christine's language warped—through the diagnosis, after she died—until a single multicolored bit of marginalia collapsed twenty years of time and friendship and contained layers of love and missing.

Pick up a book you read years ago, and you might remember what the characters were doing, what your own life was like the last time you read it, who you experienced the story with. Sometimes you leave traces of those remembered conversations—between yourself and the authors or characters, yourself and other people in your life, yourself and yourself. You might no longer know why you wrote "ahhh" or "?" or "!!!!!" in the margins. Maybe you weren't even the one who made those notes, because you got the book used, and some other reader had already left their marks on the page, so now you are in a conversation with that person, too, stretching this one text across time, place, and experience.

Any collection of words, however expressed, can invite these kinds of conversations that connect I and we, then and now, here and gone. Because every utterance is already lived in, by occupants real and imagined. Every word is ours and other people's at the same time. Every voice, a "territory shared."

In 2022, ten years after Jonnie died, Emily and the kids came to California to be with family for Christmas and spent their last night in town with us.

After dinner, we played the Name Game, which involved ripping paper into strips and writing down famous people's names for guessing. Sadie, fourteen, wore a clip-on ponytail I'd bought for a New Year's party and kept swatting it dramatically from shoulder to shoulder and speaking in a Kardashian whine. Simone and Max were on the couch in their sweats and socks. They cupped their paper strips to keep each other from cheating, and I thought of the panicked looks in their eyes the summer before, when we'd caught the two of them drinking vodka from Dixie cups, which they'd denied and then confessed. I'd been pissed but also glad, because now they were close in a new, older, trouble-making way.

We didn't play the version that Chas and I had invented with Mercy and Christine, where we guessed concepts instead of celebrities. This time, we came up with a new round where, after we'd gone through all the names a few times (once limited to one-word clues, once only gestures), we could only use sounds, no words or movements at all, to get our team to figure out who was on the slip. The whole thing got so preposterous that I had a huge laughing fit and collapsed to the floor, shrieking. Out of the corner of my eye,

I saw the bookshelf where there was a picture of Jonnie—I thought I'd seen Sadie notice it there when we made dinner. It's a close-up, his face angled down, orange hair on full display, his mouth a crooked smile. Christine is on the shelf, too. She's got a fresh hair-cut, tight on the sides, a camel-colored jacket tied around her waist. She's squinting into the sun, holding a brown bag full of books.

Writhing on the rug, I looked out the window toward the hill where we'd gathered when Jonnie's sister came home from Montana, for a service that she opened with the words "I hate this." I screamed for the game to stop so I could catch my breath, the laughter splitting me open, aware of the room in our basement directly beneath me, where Emily and Jonnie had stayed on their last visit together. The next morning, they told me that they'd been kept up half the night by mice skittering maniacally under the bed. I grabbed Emily's ankle to pull myself up from the ground. "Okay," I said finally. I reached into the bowl for a slip of paper and unfolded the next word.

In 2023, eight years after Christine died, Mercy opened the two boxes Christine had labeled "for M when I'm gone." When the boxes had first come, Mercy had glanced through the contents, taken in what was there, and then closed the flaps and stashed them deep within the basement so she wouldn't see them on her way to the washing machine. She had pushed the boxes so far from view that when Chas and I flew in to see Christine at the Carriage House and I searched Mercy's basement for evidence of Christine's existence, I hadn't seen them. I thought Christine had been cleared from the house. But Christine was there. And now, after all these years, Mercy was ready to look, to unseal the envelopes and read the words on page after page. She texted me photos of all that she found.

1. A note in nearly illegible writing: "Mercy—There's a lot of History in this box—our younger selves—So, you might be Afraid of it—memories flooding your heart + mind—♥ C

2. A print-out of the graduation speech Christine delivered the year she was invited to give the keynote address at school

3. The Bad Kitty's cremation invoice: $77 for "euthanasia 20 lbs—less"

4. A photo of The Bad

5. A black-and-white postcard of two women with only their lower legs showing under a table, wearing pantyhose and sensible pumps, one secretly touching the other's shin with the pointy toe of her shoe

6. A photo from when Christine was young and had brown hair in a sweatband, elbowing another girl out of the way, lunging for a ball

7. A ski pass from Pats Peak in New Hampshire 1977 season, with a photo of Christine, barely smiling, a bob and bangs and tortoiseshell glasses

8. A card for Mercy signed "falling again + again—falling still—on your 26th Birthday—xo C"

9. A note to Mercy: "In your arms, in your tears, in the soft kisses + rubs against my cheek, in the quiet conversation, in the silences, I have felt loved. I have felt the fragility of life + the strength of us—xo C"

"All I can say is that I am weeping," Mercy texted between the pictures.

10. Another note: "Mercy—I hope these 2 boxes don't feel like intrusions into whatever life you have now—there's sadness in the poems + misc. stuff of our lives—I have loved you more than anyone else—in my life—♥ C

There it was. The phrase they didn't say. Christine had waited a long time. Until she knew it was over. Maybe the convention she'd been refusing all along wasn't saying "I love you," but saying it only when she needed to hear it back.

"It feels like I have been excavating," Mercy texted. "I am back into the crying. (I have been so shut down for so long & now so much crying?)"

I hoped it wasn't all feeling like too much at once, for Mercy to drop back into their History, as Christine had said in her note in the box—a message sent across time. It was almost as if Christine knew that Mercy wouldn't be able to open the boxes right away, that it could be years until she was ready.

Underneath the papers and postcards, Mercy came across a thick manila envelope she'd never opened, not even when she glanced inside the boxes before.

"I thought she had burned all my letters."

It was an envelope filled with Mercy's own words. Letters from a different time, so removed from the person Mercy was now that they took on the quality of someone else's voice. She could almost read them as someone else's story. She'd thought the letters were gone. That's what Christine had told her, had told me. That she had destroyed them all. But here they were, unscathed. All those years ago, sweating in her flannel shirt, Christine had burned some of what Mercy had written to her over their seventeen years together. But not all of it. Christine had picked out the pieces that she couldn't bring herself to destroy. She made her selections, sealed them in an envelope, put them inside a box, and sent them to Mercy, to whom they now belonged.

"The word is a two-sided act," I learned from the Bakhtin Circle. "It is determined by whose word it is and for whom it is meant." Which had me thinking about the difference between what we mean and whom we mean *for*. The difference between words turned to ashes and words preserved, reincarnated.

11. A letter written with red marker where Mercy describes the
    tattoo she will get on her wrist the next day: "And I think now
    of the present tense punctuation mark I'll get etched/inked
    into my skin, of what Ondaatje writes about the shedding of
    skins; of how writing to you always feels like a way of mark-
    ing time, when words settle onto a page."

"When words settle onto a page," she said. It doesn't happen in
an instant. Words need to find their place against a backdrop, on a
page and in people's lives. And they can rearrange themselves later,
shedding old meanings, taking on new ones.

"I just found one of the last letters I wrote to her. On our 'anni-
versary of a first kiss,'" Mercy texted. "My god."

The letter was dated September 2010.

12. "And I think now of how many nights in all the seasons there
    are, over 17 years that I have sat here and written to you. How
    often I have begun with this space, the setting, the elements of
    this room. How for nearly 17 years, The Bad was on the
    couch with you or sprawled out with her belly showing on
    these hardwood floors. Sometimes the only movements in the
    room were those of sound: the fire's hiss, the flip of a page of
    a book, you reaching to select a pen and the rattle that cre-
    ates, the scrape of pen or pencil on paper. And always a sound
    I took for granted, a small breathing from The Bad in her
    stillness. I was thinking of your question this summer: what
    will I do with my hands? Under that moon, all those years
    ago, we let ourselves fall into the 'if' of this love: a smile, the
    ocean, the surprise."

The letter contained a beginning and an ending. In it, Mercy told the story of when she and Christine first came together, and she anticipated the emptiness they were heading toward, the image of Christine—what will I do with my hands?—alone. Meeting and parting. Bakhtin wrote that these threshold moments are when we glimpse the "fullness of time," when time "thickens, takes on flesh."

"She once told me," Mercy texted, "that she fell in love with me when I ran my hand along The Bad's head & spine."

You feel time in a different way when you know something is about to begin and when you sense it coming to an end. If you were to touch time at this moment, it would feel like a body, warm, a presence you could take into your arms.

13. Christine's birth certificate

Why had Christine included her birth certificate?

Maybe because it marks an ultimate beginning, the first moment of connection with the world and the people we love. "In the life that I experience from within," Bakhtin wrote, "I cannot live the events of my birth and my death. . . . The events of my birth, of my valorized being-in-the-world, and finally of my death are not accomplished in me or for me. The affective weight of my life *as a whole* does not exist for me."

A birth certificate was evidence that Christine was a being-in-the-world.

"I cannot do without the other; I cannot become myself without the other; I must find myself in the other, finding the other in me," wrote Bakhtin.

"Her desire to erase out of anger and jealousy and fear and rage was not nearly as strong as her desire to be remembered and known and held," wrote Mercy. And with that, the weight of Christine's life was back in Mercy's hands.

In the essay Christine wrote about her father's ashes, the one she performed at school to a rapt audience, she spoke in images of grief and release. Her mother's *clenched fist*, the *gesture of bravery and promise*, the look of the ashes—*glitter, gritty, delicate, piercing*—a *flash in the water*. Christine described herself in the third person, at the water's edge, glimpsing *all she could know of life-after-death*. In choosing "she" over "I," she put herself inside and outside the story at once. Maybe that fluidity is what allowed me, now, to reimagine the roles and characters. Now, Christine was the flash in the water. And there was Mercy, and the rest of us, *bent over the railing, watching and waiting, surprised by what was and couldn't be.*

Mercy has a tattoo on her inner left wrist. It's an outline of a circle, bisected by two diagonal arrows. The design was drawn from an essay one of her students wrote, inspired by an assignment in Mercy's English class. She asked her students to invent new forms of punctuation. A boy in the class designed a mark for an earlier time, when letters exchanged by lovers had to travel a great distance to arrive. He proposed an alternative to the period. It was a symbol that stamped onto the page (and later onto Mercy's body) a commitment that the emotion the lover wrote down would last until the letter was received.

This was more than a period. This was a covenant, a pledge of presence that the expressed feeling would hold, hard and fast. That despite the distance and passage of time, it wouldn't change.

It's a beautiful idea, made for a great essay, and looks good on Mercy's arm. In the end, change came. And yet, the mark endured.

Acknowledgments

When I created a document called "OPW thank you" back in 2018, it was a leap of faith, presumptuous even. I had started developing bits and pieces of this book—free-writes, stray notes on my phone, eventually a couple of chapters. But there was no telling whether I'd find my way to a coherent story, let alone someone to publish it. So I started a list, to ground myself in process and community.

Then I asked Danielle Allen if she'd look at some pages, and she generously offered to introduce me to her agent, Tina Bennett— Tina Bennett! When Tina emailed a few weeks later to say she wanted to talk, I sat down on the floor of an Oakland parking garage and cried. Tina: your indefatigable belief in this project and brilliant vision for it have made all the difference in a million ways, including the instinct to pitch Spiegel and Grau, a press founded by two women—Cindy Spiegel and Julie Grau—who've been collaborating for thirty years. When I learned that Cindy Spiegel started a PhD program in comparative literature so she could read *all the time*, we bonded over the Bakhtin sections of our bookshelves, and I prayed that she'd make an offer. From our first conversation, she was able to steer me toward the soul of this story. To everyone at Spiegel and Grau: I will be thanking you for the rest of my life. In particular, thank you to Nicole Dewey, Amy Metsch, Jess Bonet, Andy Tan-Delli Cicchi, Jackie Fischetti, Nora Tomas, and Shaya d'Ornano for your enthusiasm and for helping my book reach its readers.

Endless gratitude to my teachers, from whom I learned to experience language in all of its fullness and power: Shirley Brice Heath, Ray McDermott, Paulla Ebron, Miyako Inoue, Elliot Eisner, Chloe Garcia Roberts, Cyrus Dunham. I'm lucky to be a kind of teacher, too—beginning more than twenty years ago, when I turned down a professor job and joined the mighty newsroom of YR Media (FKA Youth Radio). Belia Mayeno Saavedra, Lauren Silverman, Sophie Simon-Ortiz, Pendarvis Harshaw, Ayesha Walker: your writing as teenagers way back then showed me a new world of expression; I learned to tell stories with you. And Rebecca Martin, you gave us all permission to write without pretense and from the heart.

Scholars Caryl Emerson, Craig Brandist, and Ken Hirschkop are responsible for some of the most influential ideas out there about the life and philosophy of Mikhail Bakhtin. They had no obligation to take my calls. That they did enriched this story in fundamental ways.

I am endlessly grateful to the friends and colleagues who were among the first I shared drafts with: Amy Standen, Chris Colin, Ike Sriskandarajah, Jon Mooallem, Julie Felner, S. Craig Watkins. And then there are those who jumped in when I'd lost my bearings: Chris (again), Aline Pereira, Peggy Orenstein, Emma Borges-Scott, Sara Sarasohn, Doug McGray, Kara Dukakis, Liz Weil, Rider Alsop, Thalia Williamson, Marianne McCune. Shawn Wen told me about the wind telephone and other vital insights. Pearl Soloff and Erika Milvy: thank you for listening. Noa Azulai, Aarohi Sheth,

Noa Kushner, Michael Lezak, Zahavah Levine, Nancy Kane: our dialogues helped keep this dream alive. Seth Miller, Ruth Bond, Ben Miller, Max Miller: you remind me how much more there is to say.

There is a special kind of intimacy that comes from writing together, which I have done with Nicole Fleetwood, pretty much nonstop, since we were in our twenties. Nicole: I have not taken a step in the journey of this project (or my life since we met) without your exquisite companionship. Nishat Kurwa: after I met Tina for the first time and it looked like there was hope for *Other People's Words*, it was you I came home to: my forever new-best-friend. I started writing with Rachel Sherman when we were baby academics drafting dissertations; all these years later, still, I am guided by your rigor and generosity. With Nicole came Monifa Porter and Sussu Laaksonen, interlocutors in a constant flow of texts and drafts, plus our writing retreat at a house with a bed in the library. A second retreat, this one solo, at a cabin where legendary music had been composed, challenged me to reach for sentences worthy of its history: thank you, Mike Krieger and Kaitlyn Krieger. Sandra Stein was there from the beginning. The wonderful Tin House Workshop came through in the end.

This book is about friendship as a great love, but it is also deeply about family. Karen Strassler is the link between the two, who introduced me to Emily and to Chas, who has responded to every version of this story and held my hand through it all.

Max Darrah, Sadie Darrah, Jeanne Darrah, Dave Robinson, Peter Darrah: thank you from the bottom of my heart for sharing your magnificent Jonnie with me, in these pages and in life. Sara Newmann: you have held everyone in your arms. Max and Sadie, you keep Jonnie in the world for all of us by being exactly, spectacularly, who you are.

David Robinson: visiting with you and Abby Jaroslow in your woodshop, with Christine's objects on every shelf and her memory alive in the timber of your voice and steadfastness of your convictions, brought a whole new dimension to this story. Jamie Hamilton, you made every decision, the small ones and the impossible ones, with a clarity and love for Christine that honored her mind through the end.

And then there is my own family. My parents and siblings taught me to treasure creativity and to love unconditionally: Judy Gruskay, Norman Soep, Judy Soep, Jenny Soep, and Andrew Soep. Roma: your imagination holds an "inner infinity" matched only by your capacity to listen, create, and seek understanding. Simone: your radiant mind, fierce support, and keen editing guided me in finding these words, and your spirit lights my days. Chas: countless times, I turned to you in doubt. "What if I can't do it?" I asked, again and again. "Just keep going," you told me. "Love is still serious, but it wants to smile," wrote Bakhtin, and I thought of you.

Emily Newmann and Mercy Carbonell: I am remembering a morning in Emily's kitchen, the three of us clearing dishes after my visit with Em and the kids, Merce down from New Hampshire to drive me to the airport. The two of you were chatting, and I closed my eyes and allowed myself to imagine what it would feel like for this book to happen, for the three of us to be in this story together. I flashed back to when we were young and felt a wave of gratitude that here we were, getting old. Thank you for trusting me with your loves and your griefs, your memories, your words, your silences, your hurts, and your laughter. Bakhtin said that Great Experience brings everything to life. Thank you for bringing everything to mine. Thank you for friendship.

Notes

1 **Itaru Sasaki bought the phone booth:** The radio show *This American Life* told the story of the "wind telephone" in 2016. Reporter Miki Meek had heard about it on a Japanese TV channel. In her beautiful account of the conversations recorded in the booth, Meek described the phone as "connected to nowhere" and translated the family members' quotes I cite here.

12 **a "conversation of the most intense kind":** Mikhail Bakhtin, *Problems of Dostoevsky's Poetics* (Minneapolis: University of Minnesota Press, 1984).

12 **An outside voice can be beckoned:** Catherine Lacey, *Biography of X* (New York: Farrar, Straus & Giroux, 2023).

23 **a "Circle" with a capital C:** Ken Hirschkop, *Mikhail Bakhtin: An Aesthetic for Democracy* (Oxford: Oxford University Press, 1999).

24 **Bakhtin was called *chudak*:** Caryl Emerson, *The First Hundred Years of Mikhail Bakhtin* (Princeton, NJ: Princeton University Press, 1997).

24 **There's a scene in the Julian Barnes novel:** Julian Barnes's 2017 novel *Noise of Time* is a fictionalized story of the composer Dmitri Shostakovich's life under Soviet terror.

25 **Together with Bakhtin, Elena and their friends:** Hirschkop, *Mikhail Bakhtin: An Aesthetic for Democracy*.

25 **There was also a well-timed review:** Bakhtin, *Problems of Dostoevsky's Poetics*, 6.

25 **"people half-dead from hunger on the streets":** Ken Hirschkop, *The Cambridge Introduction to Mikhail Bakhtin* (Cambridge: Cambridge University Press, 2021).

25 **He worked for years as an accountant:** Katerina Clark and Michael Holquist, *Mikhail Bakhtin* (Cambridge, MA: Harvard University Press, 1986).

25 **Bakhtin was routinely confined:** Clark and Holquist, *Mikhail Bakhtin*.

25 **"coincide with itself":** Caryl Emerson, "Afterword on the Dark and Radiant Bakhtin," *Slavic and East European Journal* 61, no. 2 (2017): 299–310.

26 **living in ailing bodies:** Susan Petrilli, *The Self as a Sign, the World, and the Other: Living Semiotics* (New Brunswick, NJ: Transaction Publishers, 2013).

33 **"as if it is all here":** Mikhail Bakhtin, "Selections from the Wartime Notebooks," *Slavic and East European Journal* 61, no. 2 (2017): 205.

33 **Bakhtin said that limiting ourselves:** Mikhail Bakhtin, *Discourse in the Novel* (Austin: University of Texas Press, 1981), 274.

34 **"a present moment full of itself":** Mercy Carbonell, personal correspondence, January 30, 2006.

34 **Even after a person falls silent:** Bakhtin, *Problems of Dostoevsky's Poetics*, 290.

34 **"its festival of rebirth":** This is Ken Hirschkop's translation of the final phrase that is sometimes translated as "homecoming festival"; see Hirschkop, *Cambridge Introduction to Mikhail Bakhtin*.

36 **"Every word is directed toward an answer":** Bakhtin, *Discourse in the Novel*, 280.

37 **visitors stepped into phone booths:** In 2020, the filmmaker Mohammad Gorjestani and collaborators created the *1-800 Happy Birthday* project, a website and art installation in Brooklyn, New York, to celebrate the lives of Black and Brown people killed by police or while in police custody.

39 **That last line reminded me of something:** Tzvetan Todorov, *Mikhail Bakhtin: The Dialogic Principle* (Minneapolis: University of Minnesota Press, 1984).

39 **"The word in language":** Bakhtin, *Discourse in the Novel*, 293.

42 **"It is a relationship":** Wallace Stegner, *Crossing to Safety* (New York: The Modern Library, 2002), 96.

43 **"There it was, there it is":** Wallace Stegner, *Crossing to Safety* (New York: The Modern Library, 2002), 6.

44 "No one speaks or writes straight": Emerson, *First Hundred Years of Mikhail Bakhtin*, 8.

45 Analysis of language and literature: Hirschkop, *Cambridge Introduction to Mikhail Bakhtin*.

46 "He deprived posterity of some priceless insights": Terry Eagleton, "I Contain Multitudes," *London Review of Books* 29, no. 12 (21 June 2007).

46 The students set out to salvage: Clark and Holquist, *Mikhail Bakhtin*.

47 A document was prepared: Hirschkop, *Mikhail Bakhtin: An Aesthetic for Democracy*.

47 "reverse plagiarism": Clark and Holquist, *Mikhail Bakhtin*, 150.

47 "I give myself verbal shape": Valentin Voloshinov, *Marxism and the Philosophy of Language* (Cambridge, MA: Harvard University Press, 1986), 23.

48 "I always sit on two chairs": Bakhtin, "Selections from the Wartime Notebooks," 211.

56 "In which utterance": Bakhtin, cited in Clark and Holquist, *Mikhail Bakhtin*, 170.

57 "A prose writer can distance himself": Bakhtin, *Discourse in the Novel*, 299. Note that in this quotation, there is yet another judgment call to be made about translation. Caryl Emerson and Michael Holquist use the word "materialized" to describe Bakhtin's characterization of language, but when I spoke to Ken Hirschkop about the passage, he suggested that a better term would be "embodied," or even, maybe, "enfleshed."

58 In this passage, Bakhtin starts off: From Lorrie Moore's *Who Will Run the Frog Hospital* (Knopf, 1994), where the narrator remembers a strange habit from when she was a little girl: "I wanted to make chords, to splinter my throat into harmonies. . . . It seemed like something one should be able to do, with concentration and a muscular push of air . . . to people myself" (5).

58 and Bakhtin hadn't used it: Deborah Tannen, "Talking the Dog: Framing as Interactional Resources in Family Discourse," *Research on Language and Social Interaction* 37, no. 4 (2004): 399–420. In making this point, Tannen cites a 2001 paper from Bakhtin scholars Tatiana Bubnova and M. Pierette Malcuzynski.

59 There's another ancient term: David Goldblatt, "Ventriloquism: Ecstatic Exchange and the History of the Artwork," *Journal of Aesthetics and Art Criticism* 51, no. 3 (1993): 389–98.

60 "two separate branches of humanity": Emmanuel Carrère, *Lives Other Than My Own* (New York: Picador, 2012), 19.

61 **Emily had her own writing to do:** More of Emily's writing can be found at emilynewmannwrites.com.

61 **the dungeon of a single context:** Bakhtin, *Discourse in the Novel*, 274.

72 **"Creativity," he wrote:** Clark and Holquist, *Mikhail Bakhtin*, 151.

74 **We know now that the more likely reason:** Hirschkop, *Cambridge Introduction to Mikhail Bakhtin*.

74 **Yuri had two prized possessions:** Author interview with Craig Brandist, July 18, 2018.

74 **But Bakhtin would remind us:** Clark and Holquist, *Mikhail Bakhtin*, 350.

76 **I saw a reading once:** Cord Jefferson, "Leave a Message," *Pop-Up Magazine*, live performance, The Theatre at Ace Hotel, Los Angeles, September 29, 2018.

78 **"His heart stopped":** Quoted in Sam Anderson, "Laurie Anderson Has a Message for Us Humans," *New York Times*, October 6, 2021.

79 **Bakhtin's understanding of love:** Irina Sandominskala, "Bakhtin in Bits and Pieces," *Slavic and East European Journal* 61, no. 2 (2017): 295.

84 **"The thing about a story is":** Tim O'Brien, *The Things They Carried* (New York: Houghton Mifflin Harcourt, 1990), 200.

86 **Christine had lost what Bakhtin:** Clark and Holquist, *Mikhail Bakhtin*.

87 **"A word is a bridge":** Valentin Voloshinov, *Marxism and the Philosophy of Language* (Cambridge, MA: Harvard University Press, 1986), 214.

118 **"play of light and shadow":** Bakhtin, *Discourse in the Novel*, 277.

119 **Loopholes are words:** Bakhtin, *Problems of Dostoevsky's Poetics*.

120 **"language preserves an otherwise":** Sandominskala, "Bakhtin in Bits and Pieces," 283.

138 **"In the broken rhythm":** Sandominskala, "Bakhtin in Bits and Pieces," 288.

139 **No "inner open kernel":** Bakhtin, "Selections from the Wartime Notebooks," 211.

141 **Joseph Stalin heard her play live:** "One Amazing Pianist Dared to Criticise Joseph Stalin—and Remarkably Lived to Tell the Tale," Classic FM, August 23, 2016, classicfm.com.

142 **And then there was Bakhtin's wife:** Hirschkop, *Cambridge Introduction to Mikhail Bakhtin*.

142 **"receiving the callers":** Clark and Holquist, *Mikhail Bakhtin*, 340.

142 **"I really did not know":** Bakhtin cited in Hirschkop, *An Aesthetic for Democracy*, 128.

146 **"dreams of her mother":** Natasha Trethewey, *Memorial Drive* (New York: Harper Collins, 2020), 73.

147   "There is nothing to do": Ingrid Rojas Contreras, *The Man Who Could Move Clouds* (New York: Doubleday, 2022).

148   "Alice looked back": Marjorie Williams, "The Halloween of my Dreams," *The Washington Post,* November 3, 2004, washingtonpost .com.

148   "One of the things that makes": "One Last Thing before I Go," September 23, 2016, *This American Life*, podcast, thisamericanlife.org.

148   the absence of "I love you": For more on this idea, see Jonathan Safran Foer, "A Primer for the Punctuation of Heart Disease," *New Yorker,* June 2, 2002, newyorker.com.

149   a "blow" and a "gift": Bakhtin, "Selections from the Wartime Notebooks," 209.

155   "the fear of the immeasurable": Mikhail Bakhtin, *Rabelais and His World* (Bloomington: Indiana University Press, 1984), 335.

155   "I imagined the two of them": Carrère, *Lives Other Than My Own.*

158   "I like the idea of my friends": The Response, "Four Cartoonists on What They Want to Happen to Their Bodies," *Nib*, October 5, 2018, thenib.com.

166   "the realm of maximal freedom": Emerson, *First Hundred Years of Mikhail Bakhtin*, 128.

170   When I found a line: Jennifer Senior describes a similar process in her 2021 Atlantic story, "What Bobby McIlvaine Left Behind." She calls it "literary resurrection."

171   "And there is no such thing": Slav N. Gratchev, "Bakhtin in His Own Voice: Interview by Victor Duvakin: Translation and Notes by Slav N. Gratchev," *College Literature* 43, no. 3 (Summer 2016): 592–602.

172   "territory shared": Voloshinov, *Marxism and the Philosophy of Language.*

177   "The word is a two-sided act": Voloshinov, *Marxism and the Philosophy of Language.*

179   "fullness of time": Mikhail Bakhtin, *Forms of Time and of the Chronotope in the Novel* (Austin: University of Texas Press, 1981), 146.

179   "thickens, takes on flesh": Bakhtin, *Forms of Time and of the Chronotope in the Novel*, 84.

179   "In the life that I experience from within": Bakhtin, cited in Todorov, *Mikhail Bakhtin: The Dialogic Principle*, 56.

179   "I cannot do without the other": Bakhtin, *Problem of Dostoevsky's Poetics*, 287.

182   one of her students: Mercy's student who designed the punctuation mark that became her tattoo was Alex Fankuchen.

About the Author

Lissa Soep started a career in audio storytelling more than twenty years ago after she finished a PhD at Stanford, turned down an academic job, and joined Youth Radio (now YR Media), a nonprofit newsroom in Oakland, California. She has produced award-winning radio stories for NPR and other outlets that have advanced reforms in juvenile justice and child welfare, and since 2020, she has edited narrative podcasts with Vox Media and established a learning and speaker series for aspiring and veteran audiomakers. She lives in San Francisco.